D0948426

Where the River
Bends

Where the River Bends

A Memoir by
Barry Raine

Ontario Review Press
PRINCETON, NEW JERSEY

Ontario Review Press

Copyright © 2002 by Barry Raine

ALL RIGHTS RESERVED

Distributed by W. W. Norton & Company, Inc.
500 Fifth Avenue, New York, NY 10110

Library of Congress Cataloging-in-Publication Data

Raine, Barry.
Where the river bends: a memoir / Barry Raine. — 1st ed.
p. cm.
ISBN 0-86538-104-6 (alk. paper)
1. Rape—Louisiana—New Orleans. 2. Rape
victims—Louisiana—New Orleans. I. Title.

HV6568.N46 R35 2002
364.15'32'092—dc21
[B]   2001052344

Design and composition by Tim Jones

MANUFACTURED IN THE UNITED STATES OF AMERICA

FIRST EDITION

For my mother, Elise

And for my sister, Andrea
IN MEMORIAM
1966–2001

Where the River

Bends

One

THE NIGHT OF THE RAPE is a typical New Orleans night when, even in October, you can break a sweat standing still well after the sun goes down. My friends Catherine and Alex and my brother Paul, and I, are sitting at dusk along Audubon Park's promenade that juts out over the east bank of the Mississippi River. This is a spot called the Butterfly because of a large pink concrete sculpture. Two slabs opposing each other arch into the air—a huge pink butterfly poised at the edge of the churning, brown Mississippi. From this spot, the view is wide and distant over the notoriously treacherous waters. About fifteen feet below us are marshy banks overgrown with the drooping, sinewy branches of swamp willows and thick, five-foot reeds. Over the treetops, we can see freighters and tankers as they either head out to sea or come into the port.

For me, a local born and raised here, it is just an ordinary Saturday night after another monotonous day. I have a part-time job selling men's shoes at a suburban department store. It is 1981 and

I am a sophomore in college, biding my time until I leave the following summer for a year of school in Rome. I have never been out of the United States before. I spend much of my time here at the river, dreaming of my Italian days, watching flocks of clumsy brown pelicans lift off and then dive for fish.

The Mississippi, that cuts a nearly 2,500-mile swath from northern Minnesota to the Gulf of Mexico, is most formidable here at New Orleans, where its depth and width make every New Orleanian respectful of the river's power and presence and its ability to decimate the city given the right conditions. Every child raised in the city is warned that swimming in the Mississippi is forbidden. If you do it, parents say, you will probably never come out. Legendary eddies and undertows, known to ship captains for making the waters in the port so difficult to navigate, are like vacuum hoses. Within a few feet of the shore, the whirlpools will supposedly suck under even the most powerful swimmers and, indeed, have claimed many lives. Here, the river dominates, and local geography terms are always coined in relation to "the east bank," "the west bank," or "across the river." I was born here. I respect the Mississippi.

"DIDN'T YOU think my dad seemed nervous when we left the house?" Catherine asks me. I hadn't noticed. All her father had said was that the park was a better place to hang out than a sleazy bar, as though convinced we were really headed to one because that's where he would have gone if given the choice.

Catherine is from a genteel Southern family, the youngest of eight children. She wants to become a potter, and has just gotten her own potter's wheel. She emulates late 60's dress: sporting long batik, billowy skirts, going barefoot most of the time, wearing sandals when shoes are required. Most endearing to me are her sudden bursts of wild laughter that erupt without warning.

First, she'll shriek after a silent funny thought, then her knees buckle, and then she's in a heap on the ground, shoulders moving up and down in spasms.

Catherine and her father, Hugh, have introduced me to opera. He has taught me about the composers, the stories of their lives, as well as who all the great singers are. Before meeting him, the only opera singer I'd ever heard of was Mario Lanza, who my mother claimed once cracked a glass with a high note. No one knows, not even Catherine, that for the past few years her father has been my primary role model. I am 19. I am looking for a guide. My own father is uneducated, uninterested in learning, negative.

TONIGHT ALEX and Catherine had shown up at the apartment I share with my brother, Paul, who is on leave from Vassar College in upstate New York, getting job experience before he returns to finish in the spring. Alex is an acquaintance of Paul's and has lived as a street kid for years in New Orleans, hustling both men and women, and doing whatever else he needs to in order to survive. Alex is no one any of our parents would approve of.

We all had climbed into Alex's pickup truck and meandered through the streets of the Garden District until we hit the curving roads of Audubon Park. We drove into the park through a great vault of oak trees, roaming until we found a spot a few feet from a steep trail that wound down to the water's edge.

We have been lucky to get such a choice location on a Saturday night, but Alex knows places like this where few people venture—out of sight and range of the park police.

We settle down to listen as Catherine plays classical Spanish songs on her banana-wood guitar, and soon we fall into a pleasant, humidity-induced lethargy. When I turn around to reach for the bottle of wine we've brought, I spot a black man fifty yards in the distance, walking along the sidewalk, passing another gathering of people who are now beginning to fold up their blankets and head home. He walks very slowly, almost as if he is floating.

I try to dismiss the sense of a potential intrusion for a minute or so, but something compels me to glance once again back toward him. Then I realize with a shock that he is standing over us, less than two feet away from Catherine who is facing away from him, still strumming her guitar.

In the South, in a city as racially polarized as New Orleans, blacks and whites do not often mix. And it is more rare to be approached by a black stranger while you are sitting in a group of all white people in a park in the city's fanciest, and of course all-white, neighborhood.

For many white Southerners, there is an often complicated response in encounters with black people. In my case, I had one parent—my father—who was a racist and whose parents were racists and who had made bigoted remarks ever since I could remember. Yet I had a mother who fought prejudice—in particular, my father's prejudice—and who, as an adolescent girl, was ostracized by a group of her friends for insisting on riding in the back of the Saint Charles Avenue trolley car with the black people. I'd witnessed numerous nasty exchanges about race between my parents. I remembered their argument when my father discovered my mother regularly served lemonade on a tray with *our* glasses to the sweating black workers who picked up the neighborhood's garbage.

The man says his name is Zachariah. Paul, always jovial and fast on his feet, is talking to him, trying to be humorous. Paul is alarmed, but only I can see it. Zachariah's dialect is the heavy street language you can hear drifting under the twin spans of the Mississippi River bridges, where some of the poorest blacks live in the Fisher Housing Projects, just blocks away from gentrify-

4

ing, predominantly white Algiers Point. His words slur from whatever drug he has taken. I have trouble hearing what he says. But the fast pulse of my heart is also charging through my ears in a kind of thundering quiet. The scene looks as though the plot of a silent thriller is unfolding and I am a part of it. Now Catherine is looking up at him, talking. She doesn't laugh. Then she glances at me. She looks alarmed.

He crouches down in order to be eye level with us; his face is afflicted with pink scars and his big, bloodshot eyes bore into us. "Wanna buy some coke?" he says, gesturing to a bulge on his left ankle, supposedly the stash. "Wanna buy some coke?" He addresses my brother. Paul attempts to humor him, laughs, and says, "No, we can't afford it. We don't have any money." By Paul's face I can see that an alarm is surging through him, too, and he's trying not to show it.

Suddenly, Zachariah jumps to his feet, gripping a .38 pistol that he's taken from the bulge where the cocaine is supposed to have been. He demands all of our money. We automatically stand up and empty our pockets. He snatches Catherine's big straw purse from the ground and rummages through it. Then he goes completely still for a moment and yells, "Fuck!" His eyes gleam maniacally as he pulls out from Catherine's bag another .38 caliber revolver. I am stunned. I never knew she carried a gun. Zachariah dangles it from his index finger. "What the shit is this, girl!" he screams at Catherine, looking as if he wants to strangle her. Only seconds ago, she had had the power to reach in, pull out the gun and kill him. If she had done this, or if I had known about the gun her father had given her for self-protection, and I had drawn it, this whole ordeal would now have a different ending.

I have always told myself that I would know how to respond if I were ever attacked. I have almost looked forward to the chance to prove what I would do. My plan has been foolproof—until now when I'm facing two cocked .38 caliber pistols.

Zachariah orders us to lie face down on the ground. He grabs Catherine, pointing the gun at her head, and marches her to the cab of the truck. Knowing he can't see me, I turn my head to watch him. "Take off your pants, baby," he requests in mock politeness. "You ever touch a black man before? You give head?" Catherine says, "No, I've never had a black man before." He then reaches to the elastic band of her panties, pulls them down. "Leave her alone," I growl. He jerks away from her, steps out of the truck and stalks over to me, waving a gun. His eyes are glazed. He shoves the barrel into my cheek and the cold metal stings. "Shut up. One more word and you dead." I turn away and close my eyes. I hear the sounds of his footsteps returning to the truck. I'm trying to hear if he is doing anything to her, but all I can hear is whispering.

At last, I hear from above me, "Take off your clothes!" Zachariah is standing over us now, and I look up at him and I can see Catherine's vacant expression. The gun is still trained on her head. "Take off your clothes!" Zachariah orders Paul, Alex, and me. "Throw 'em on the ground! And start walkin." He tells us to walk single file down the trail to the edge of the water and into the marshy thicket of tall reeds and swamp willows. One gun is cocked and trained on Catherine's head—is it her own? The other is pointing at us. As we walk, I look up and see the tops of the trees and think, somebody will hear him if he pulls the trigger, so maybe he won't, maybe he'll just steal all our belongings and leave us.

Then we are standing at the water's edge, looking out into the menacing currents. He gathers our clothes and throws them into the knee-deep, shoreline marsh that precedes the open water. "Awright, lie down," he says, prompting us with the cold muzzle of the gun. Alex gestures to the gold chain around his neck. "Here, this is worth $400. Take it. Just let us go, man."

Zachariah shakes his head. "On the ground!"

But Alex has other ideas. "Here." He unclasps the chain and tosses it into the muck, and for a second, the potential loss of a valuable object attracts Zachariah's attention. A moment later Alex bolts, dodging the trees and running away along the water.

"Stop, mother-fucker!" Zachariah cries after him. And then he fires the gun. The shots explode, but Alex keeps running. Miraculously he gets away. "Mother-fucker!" screams Zachariah. I hope for a second that he will leave us when he realizes that Alex is going for help. But, no; incensed, he grabs Catherine by her right arm, wrenches it, and pushes her to the ground. "Any of you get up and she's dead," he says to us, gesturing to the .38 pointed at Catherine's head.

He tells her to lie on her back and puts her feet flat on the ground. He bends her knees, spreads her legs, and with the barrel of the still-cocked .38 grinding into her neck, he unsnaps his pants with one hand, pushes them down over his ass, pulls out his erect brown penis and repositions her legs one more time. I can't help noticing that because he wants to keep the gun embedded in her neck, it is more difficult for him to enter her. But somehow he does and, desperate and enraged, I helplessly watch how he manages to get his face inches from hers and how she keeps her eyes wide open, trained on him. I can see the dark brown cheeks of his ass, underscored by his rumpled pants moving up and down between her legs. He keeps trying to adjust his hips so that he can slide in more easily. He ends up halfway on his side, leaning on one arm. He does not make a sound, and she lies there passive to his violation. Though she keeps silence, Catherine never stops looking at him.

I had been taught the standards by which manhood is measured. I had been taught the self-sacrificing role a man must play when faced with protecting women. It is a code of honor, an unbendable rule in the South. And if you live outside of this rule, you risk losing the respect of other men. My instant reaction is not only shame of my impotence to help, but beyond that, that she is a white woman being raped by a black man. And no matter what anybody says, how liberal or how conservative my upbringing might have been, I have grown up in the South and I know this racial difference between Catherine and her assailant will bring a new level of meaning to the crime-in-progress.

Suddenly, Zachariah pulls out of Catherine and jumps to his feet. He comes over to me and snaps his pants in front of my face, forcing me to see the single, viscous white strand of semen dripping from the head of his penis. As fast as he had wrenched her to the ground, he now seems to have forgotten about her.

It is dark now, and my body is completely wet from the lapping water of the Mississippi. Zachariah points one of the .38s at Paul and me, making mock gunshot sounds, as he pretends to shoot each of us. "POW! BANG!," he yells, laughing a snarling laugh. He approaches me again, and slams the toe of his cheap loafers into my genitals. The systemic pain is an instant, agonizing surprise. My legs draw up, my knees are pulled to my chest, as the burning, wrenching nausea boils up from the bottom of my groin and shoots into my abdomen. My reaction is to turn on my side and curl into the fetal position, to clutch my abdomen as tightly as I can to try to make the pain stop. I feel like I have to vomit and cry at the same time. I keep moving around, and Paul whispers, "Stop moving, Barry. Be still."

"What's that?" Zachariah says to him. "You got something to say to me, boy?"

"No," says Paul and Zachariah kicks him where he's kicked me.

Still woozy from the pain, now hearing my brother's agonies, I fantasize that Alex will come rushing back any minute, a battery of police officers and patrol cars with him, lights flashing, to save us. They will capture Zachariah and invite us to torture him until he is in agony, and until we kill him.

But he tells the three of us to stand up and walk into the marsh and to keep walking out into the river until we are told to stop. He must know how dangerous this is, he must know that we could be sucked down and drowned. We hesitate and he waves the gun once again.

The water is black, the moon enshrouded by a layer of fog. To make sure we keep moving out into the river, he uncocks the gun and then cocks it again. The metal chambers give off a deadly click. We wade past the piles of our clothes that are now floating in the brown muck. We push the low-hanging willow branches from in front of our faces and begin to step into the shallows. At first our feet sink into the muddy bottom, but soon the increasing depth of the water makes us more buoyant. With each uncertain step we take, we sink less and less into the muck until we are nearly floating.

I can't help thinking that tomorrow this will be a story in the *The Times-Picayune*: the tale of a group of idiots going to the park and getting wild enough to take off their clothes, the story of a group of kids who decided they'd be the first in history to make it across the Mississippi and who swam until the undertow got them. And Zachariah will come, with his gun strapped on one ankle and Catherine's in his pocket and watch as they pull our bodies from the water.

Paul, who is just ahead of me, stops wading. This is the point where we have to start swimming, to choose between dying by drowning or dying from a bullet. He seems to be weighing each grim alternative. And then he ventures to turn around and his look of terror turns to bewilderment. "He's gone," Paul says. "He's gone!"

I want to race to the shore, to flee the danger of the current, but Catherine, walking beside me, clearly needs help. She can barely walk. She has slipped away from herself, from us. Her shoulders are sagging, and she is crying softly.

Shouldering Catherine, my brother and I begin wading against the strong current toward the shore. In the darkness we manage to find our clothes, wet and caked with mud, and get dressed. I want to put my arms around Catherine, but I hold back because I feel that I have failed her, that I should have risked being killed, that I should have been able to pull him off her somehow. Even though he'd held a gun to her throat and might have pulled the trigger, the code of honor says I should have somehow intervened, even if it meant dying to save a woman from being raped.

There is a chill in the air. But the air is warm, so the coolness must be a part of a nervous delirium. So much has been altered in these last few minutes, so much forfeited, so much stripped away.

BY THE TIME we climb up the path from the river, it's dark and we are shivering as we stand in a huddle high above the water, Paul and I trying to protect Catherine with our arms around her shoulders.

Then a car rounds the bend of the empty park road, heading straight toward us. We see it almost like a mirage, a vision drifting toward us through the waves of heat spiraling up from the macadam of the parking lot. Paul and I instinctively move toward the car and begin waving our hands to summon help. It's just dark enough that the car should put on headlights, but it is running without them and continues towards us. We race out onto the long wing of the Butterfly's parking lot. The person driving finally sees us, slows down, but doesn't stop and then begins to pass by.

Paul and I glance at one another, incredulous. We vaguely realize that perhaps the person driving thinks we're crazy, drunken youths on the ambush. I'm about to say this to Paul, as I'm looking to see who's driving, whether it's a man or a woman, hopefully a young person who might stop if we implore him. And then the strange, nightmare vision makes me doubt my own eyes. It's Zachariah.

At first it doesn't make sense. Wouldn't he be trying to run us over, wouldn't he be drawing his gun to fire at our disobedience? Wouldn't he even stop to make us think he was going to help us and then put us away forever? But no, he just looks at us, impassively, as though we are no longer worth his while, and continues driving through the parking lot. Then we distinctly hear a ripple of his laughter, and through the rearview mirror I can see the reflection of the smile on his face.

Two

As though precisely timed to Zachariah's departure, another car rounds the bend: the Audubon Park police. From the passenger side, Alex jumps out, still wearing only his red bikini underwear. He streaks towards us, screaming, "Whew, I'm glad ya'll are all right. I ran my ass off fast as I could." He had continued to run at full speed all the way down the long hill from the river until he found the park security officer who had picked him up and brought him back to us.

Alex looking desperately for a cop is ironic. Since he started breaking the law at fourteen, he has had many encounters with the police. He's spent a few years in juvenile detention centers for various petty crimes, much of the time in solitary confinement because of bad behavior. He filled those solo hours with marathon sets of thousands of pushups and situps, hours of determined running in place until he had calculated he had run about fifteen to twenty miles at a stretch several times a week.

By the time he was released at 15, Alex realized that his perfectly sculpted physique, his blue eyes, and his cocky, tough-guy demeanor could make him some sex money if he played the streets of major cities the way he'd played the house of detention guards for favors. He hitchhiked his way to New Orleans. Attractive as much to men as to women, he often made $150 per hour from both sexes. After a few months in New Orleans, Alex had been wily enough to sleep with some of the city's ranking married businessmen but his growing reputation came to the attention of the New Orleans Police Department vice squad. He was arrested once and since then has managed to elude any new charges while perpetrating his business.

It is no surprise that Alex had been the only one among us to see the only split-second chance for escape—and to seize it. He has an acute sense of danger. He has already pulled himself out of many life-threatening situations.

Several seconds after Alex finds us, two New Orleans Police Department cars roar across the railroad tracks, bouncing hard as they race up the hill, lights flashing and sirens wailing as they skid to a stop right before us. By now, the Butterfly is empty—everyone having disappeared as soon as the sun slipped away—and a light, low veil of fog is moving onshore from the river, signifying another hot day for tomorrow.

Stupefied by blue lights of the patrol cars, we answer routine questions while the cops write on crime report forms attached to clipboards. Alex is watching the police warily, whispering that he recognizes some, praying that they don't recognize him. Raspy police radios broadcasting locations of crimes in progress are interrupted by foghorn blasts from passing tankers.

More police vehicles arrive including a shiny station wagon belonging to the rape squad. A tall raw-bone looking man confers with some of the police and then slowly approaches Catherine and introduces himself. They confer quietly for a minute or so,

Catherine nodding her head. Her shoulders seem to slump more and more as she speaks to him. Finally she comes over and explains that he is a detective who will be taking her to Charity Hospital's emergency room. I offer to come, but the man has already told her that I will soon be taken directly to the police station. And so, I watch Catherine being led away to the station wagon. The detective holds the door open for her, she climbs in and they drive away. I bid her goodbye, feeling hollow and worn, wondering how long it will be until I get to see her again.

Then Paul, Alex and I are riding in the back seat of the patrol car, behind the wire mesh screen that separates the criminals from the cops. The officer behind the wheel makes the turn from Audubon Park onto St. Charles Avenue and we drive down the nighttime grandeur of New Orleans' most exclusive residential street, passing its many darkened mansions. I start to wonder how I'm going to tell my father what has happened. When I was growing up, he'd always told me a real "he-man" should be able to defend himself against anybody as long as the other guy fought fair. But wielding a gun wasn't "fair." Nevertheless, I know what he's going to say. Gun or no gun, "You mean not one o' da tree of ya couldn't've rapped him one?"

My father was once a street fighter and an amateur boxer who had unfailing confidence in his ability to conquer anyone he set out to fight. To him, other men with gracious manners, especially "college men" with a fondness for books, are wimps. But to me intellect and grace, which Catherine's father has, are assets, not shortcomings. But can Hugh be expected to understand? After all this is his daughter who has been violated. He is the one who has spoken to me so much about a man's duty, who has described the code of Southern honor in terms of the role men must play as protectors of women.

The officer driving the patrol car, almost as if he senses that I'm thinking this, breaks the long silence. "Lemme set you straight on somethin'," he says. "Y'all alive, right? You got away from him. So y'all done the right thing. And you're going to have to remember that every time someone asks you what went on."

Nevertheless, sitting with my brother and Alex in back, I grow more and more convinced that Catherine's father and my father and every other man who will ever hear about this will look at my brother and me and will wonder how we could ever have let this happen.

TULANE AVENUE is, arguably, the ugliest street in New Orleans. It's a several-mile-long seedy strip of cheap motels, adult bookstores, and barrooms that stink of old beer and teem with panhandlers and whores. It is lined by half-dead palm trees, their tattered brown fronds rustling in the traffic fumes. It is one of the city's longest streets, and for block upon block signs are posted along the median, prohibiting U-turns and even left turns. New Orleans played a cruel joke on drivers when it made the traffic laws for Tulane Avenue: you must keep driving for what seems like miles until you are permitted to turn left legally to head back to where you came from. The legal alternative is to exit right anywhere you choose onto one of the despairing, hopeless ghetto streets that surround the criminal courts building and the police station.

The patrolman now leads the way into a building, garishly lighted by bright fluorescent tubes. The corridors echo with ringing phones, with the yells of the accused and their accusers, with the sirens of police cruisers arriving in the garage, and with the laughter of policemen who seem immune to all the tension. Criminals in handcuffs, newly arrested, shuffle recalcitrantly down the halls, trying to make the job more difficult for the patrolmen escorting them. And victims mill through the maze of passageways waiting to tell their stories.

One man has been beaten severely, and his face and clothes are spattered with blood. A well-dressed, attractive, middle-aged woman, with a bandage across her jaw and a well-padded gauze patch taped across an eye, is still wearing a frozen look of surprise and terror. As we round a corner, a flimsy metal double door flies open and four patrolmen burst through it, leading an enormous black woman, about six feet tall, very fat and in handcuffs, down the hall. Wearing a dirty tan house dress and hightop basketball sneakers with torn backs that show her calloused, naked heels, she is flailing, kicking and trying to bite them. The cops stop and wrestle her up against the wall so they can attach ankle chains to prevent her kicking. All the while, she spews a deep, guttural string of threats and expletives.

The officer leading us through the corridors looks at us conspiratorially and smirks. He explains that that particular woman is always in trouble for petty crimes, a "repeat visitor" as he calls her whom the courts have continued to free on technicalities. "We bring Ernestine in here every time she changes her drawz. And it makes her mad. So we throw 'er in a cell till she calms huself down. This time, we caught Nessy sellin' dope to kids and carryin' concealed."

Farther down, two officers are handcuffing a man who is alternately screaming "You got the wrong guy, man, I didn't do nothin'" and then, a few seconds later, congratulating himself for pummeling his girlfriend: "the bitch deserved it. She got what she was looking fuh!" A young woman who looks no more than 18 stands crying in a hallway. A large hole has been ripped from the back of her blouse, and she is wearing only one shoe and her arms are skinned and bruised. By the time we reach the end of the long corridor, we've learned that we're nothing special.

Finally we enter a large common waiting room that has the feeling of a holding pen, overflowing with people sitting in too-small, hard white plastic chairs, shifting their weight as they try to make themselves more comfortable. Are they waiting to report a crime, or are they waiting to hear the fate of a friend or a family member who also happens to be a criminal? All of the chairs are taken, so people are sitting on the floor, their backs against the wall, wearing faces of grief, impatience, trauma, shock. The room is like a clearinghouse for every innocent life that happened to be in the path of a random act of violence. And soon we, too, are sitting on the floor, backs against the wall. Just a few hours have passed since we became another crime statistic. Our old lives, our pre-attack lives, are now recurring to us, reminding us of who we were. I look around at all the people we have seen, and at ourselves, and I think of houses blasted to pieces by tornadoes. There is something as impersonal and as devastating as a tornado about the aftermath of a criminal act such as this.

Tonight, as usual, the humidity is high, and it seeps through the walls from the foul curbsides of Tulane Avenue. Our patrolman has already told us that the worst nights, the most homicidal nights, are Friday nights like this one, with air so heavy you can see it form rings around the streetlights. On nights like this one, the blood of New Orleans comes to a bubbling boil. At least an hour goes by before our names are finally called.

The sergeant's office is not furnished for comfort. His chairs are straight-backed, metal, with hard green vinyl cushions. His floor is made of unforgiving tile, hard as concrete. His tables and his desk are metal or imitation wood. His lamps blind more than they illuminate. Welcoming us, his greeting is warm. He offers us coffee from a sludge-encrusted old Bunn-o-Matic coffee maker. The coffee looks and tastes like bitter brown water.

He directs us to a long, rectangular metal table at the far end of his office. On top of it are several large spiral binders that look hundreds of pages thick. These contain plastic photo album sheets filled with mug shots. "These books are our bibles," says the sergeant. "If the guy is in here, that means he has a record, used to be in jail, and now he's out. Most of 'em wind up commitin' more crimes and they wind up back in jail. Study the pictures. Study 'em, and then look at 'em again, and triple check 'em, and before you say you recognize one of 'em, be as sure as you can that you got the right guy. Awright?"

The plastic pages offer us a sea of possible faces to examine. Most of these men look rather scruffy, though benign; a sinister, threatening face is the exception rather than the rule. The pictures are grouped in the binder corresponding to the crimes committed—murder, armed robbery, rape. Some of these faces make me shudder when I imagine what they may have done to their victims.

As I flip through the sheets, I am waiting to see the face of "our guy." ("Your guy" is what the police have begun to call the man who has just attacked us.) We saw him up close, and for a long time, so there is no way that we won't recognize him. Midnight strikes. It is now five hours since the crime by the river. We have given our statements, answered too many questions, poured over dozens of mug shots, while replaying many times what happened. I wonder how we will ever find him, how will they ever prove it was him.

Then the sergeant emerges from his office and, in the shadow of his bright, institutional light, asks Paul, Alex and me how we are doing with the pictures, have we found anyone who looks familiar? Growing discouraged, and becoming aware of how hard it must be to capture criminals when there are so many on the books, we continue to turn the pages, studying every mug shot, as we become more determined not to give up. We are not to speak to one another, he reminds us, and when and if we think we see someone who fits the rapist's description, we are to proceed into the office next door and tell him in private. About thirty minutes after he walks away, Paul stands up and enters the detective's office. Soon after, Alex follows, and then I approach. And within the next twenty minutes, we will learn that the three of us identified the same young man. And that we are all adamant in our belief that we have identified the man who attacked us.

In the photograph, the suspect wears a patchy beard, there are deep cuts on his forehead, nose, and cheeks, and dried blood spots on his face. His skin is severely pock-marked, his hair braided into cornrows. He wears a stained brown and beige shirt. When I study the face, I see his eyes are bloodshot, not menacing or cold, but far away. He hardly looks threatening. But it is the same blank, seemingly harmless gaze that concealed what he would do in the next several minutes after he'd first approached us in the park. It is the same face of the man who told me he'd kill me if I tried to interfere with him, the same face of the man driving the tan Chrysler Cordoba. One by one, we enter the office to tell the sergeant without hesitation or doubt that we can identify the suspect.

Signaling to his deputy to bring in someone from the hallway, the sergeant says, "I have someone I want y'all to meet."

A tall, buxom woman with bleached blonde hair "teased high into an unruly nest," as my brother later described it, is escorted into the room where we are waiting. She's wearing tight Gloria Vanderbilt jeans on which she has embroidered her own floral designs, and an orange strapless elasticized tube top that squeezes around her chest and upper back and barely covers her large breasts. Several cheap gold chains and necklaces hang around her neck, and the huge white hoop earrings, three rings on each hand, and white high-gloss fingernail polish that match her chalky white lipstick complete her ensemble. The skin on her cheeks hangs heavy with flaking powder and too much rouge.

"This is Marla Boudreaux," the sergeant says. "The suspect broke into her apartment tonight, and we think he was on his way home from the park where he had just left you."

Marla pushes herself into the middle of the room. "I tole the sergeant here, when I heard what happened to ya'll an that ya'll were here, that it hadda be the same guy in my house that came to the park. My heart broke I felt so bad. "

The sergeant begins to explain how they had captured Zachariah in her apartment an hour or so ago, but then Marla interjects, not impolitely, insistent upon recounting in her own words what happened in her living room a few hours before.

"Ah was just gettin home from the barroom, where I had been workin' a double since early in the mornin," Marla explains in her deep Alabama twang. "I open up the gate to the alley that leads to ma door and all, an' this guy comes up to me from nowheres and pulls a gun out of his pants and cocks it and points it at my head and tells me he's comin' in to rob me."

She explains that she comes from northern Alabama, where she learned not only what a gun looked like, but how to identify them by size and make. So she knows he was pointing a .38 and is well aware of the damage a .38 can do. She assures us that she is a pretty good shot, herself. She pauses to light another cigarette off the one she has in her mouth. I'm amazed that she seems so calm, relaying the story in a matter-of-fact tone, without a hint of emotion. The threats on her life from an armed man in her house sound more like a bother or an inconvenience than a trauma. She tells the story with the same composure as if she were talking about an unwelcome acquaintance who had dropped by and had then gotten out of hand.

"So," she continues, "he motions to me—now, I gotta tell ya— I gotta be fair to say he wudn't bein' mean or nothin'—to be quiet and go in the house. So we get inside the house and he tells me I gotta lay on the floor with 'im and he says he waunts to talk about god and stuff, an' I can only imagine what's gonna come next. So, I did, and then when I was on the floor I seen he had another gun strapped to 'is laig." She began to wonder what his interests were, money or her, but no matter what they were, he was likely to kill her, and she was trying to figure out what would be the most enjoyable way to spend her last hour.

She is a great raconteur and by now we are all listening to every word, riveted by her recollection and straining to hear if he raped her. My brother, in particular, is enthralled. He loves hard-bitten women who live on the fringes of society. I can tell he likes her tartness, her salty talk, her "don't fuck with me, mister" attitude. Surely aware of her rapt audience, she fluffs and pats her hair with one hand, then, giving her cigarette to the other hand, she pats the other side approvingly. "So, I ask him, I say to him, 'Look, honey, if you gonna kill me, all I want is to get me a cold burr and just sip it down good before I go and meet ma maker.' And then I says to him 'I can git you one, too, if you waunt. You waunt salt on the rim, hon?'" She recalls how at first Zachariah seemed too stoned to react to her, but that he didn't object when she slowly got up off the floor and went to the kitchen to get the beer. He didn't notice her duck out of sight to call the police.

"I don't know how he was with ya'll, but with me he didn't seem to wanna do nuthin'. He was like not movin' and he seemed real out of it." That was when she started to think that she had more of a chance than she realized to overpower him if she could figure out how. She remembered that before leaving for work, she'd put a cold six pack in the freezer to get the beer even colder, and had forgotten about them. "When I opened up the freezer, they was froze solid. Hard as a stone, all of 'em, you know what I mean? So, I took two of 'em outta there, like I was gonna give one to 'im. I walk back into the living room. But right then I seen two police officers standin' outside the winda. And then he sees 'em and points his gun right at 'em. So, I take ma can and whack 'im on the head, and he was knocked out cold. And then I grabbed them guns and let the police in."

The officers cuffed Zachariah, and when he woke up, half dazed, they started leading him out of the building. But he became violent and, though handcuffed, managed to break free and ended up diving through Marla's window onto the sidewalk. The officers raced outside and grabbed him and he fought them viciously and kicked both of them as they were shoving him into the back of the patrol car. Later on, when they searched him, they found some of our credit and identification cards.

My brother laughs. I can tell he is thrilled with the story, amused and fascinated how this "tart" as he later called her (and who by now was very taken with his flirtations) had been held captive and had knocked out her captor with a can of beer. Paul's reaction makes me angry. And I can't believe she had been alone with Zachariah, with no other witnesses and no one else to help her and had somehow been able to subdue him. Her conquest of Zachariah sounds so easy, so simple to accomplish with a frozen can of Dixie beer. Was he really so stoned in her apartment that he was useless, compared to how he had been much earlier in the night when he was just getting started? Nevertheless, she stopped him and we had not. And that fact eats away at me. "Three guys against one—gun or no gun . . ." I can hear my father's words. Yes, it is a relief that Zachariah has been captured. But now I dread the moment Marla Boudreaux's story will make its way into the newspaper.

Three

WHAT I DID NOT WANT to think about was the reaction of my father and of Catherine's father.

My father was a repairman for the telephone company. A laborer all of his life, he was active in the powerful labor union within South Central Bell, which was especially volatile and high-profile during the many strikes that were called in the 1950s. He hated "scabs." When he saw "scabs" or had solid proof that people had crossed the picket line, he would find out who they were, track them down, and, with his friend Hugo, another union activist, beat them senseless. My dad liked to tell tales of barroom brawls. Even though he didn't drink, he liked to say, "anybody who looked cross-eyed at me, pow, I rapped 'em one in the face." He recalled fights in painstaking detail, and remarked how sometimes he and Hugo would each take on two guys at once. Then he would recite what injuries each person suffered and who had won which round. He'd show me his huge hands and boast how much damage they'd done, how many skulls and chests they'd battered. And yet, in all of his stories of victory, he always gave Hugo, his idol, more of the glory than he gave himself. I would ultimately learn that it was apocryphal, his claim to have been one of the most feared men in New Orleans. His machismo was actually a flimsy shell that did little to protect his fragile core.

My first memory of my father's power is my fourth birthday party on a New Orleans afternoon in May. He is towering over me. I am sitting at the picnic table under the huge swamp willow tree. Several of the neighborhood kids have gathered for one of the lavish birthday parties my mother took pains to give us, though we could not always afford it. My father is showing off the blue model airplane that he has assembled for my birthday present. He is a strapping six-foot-four, well over two hundred solid pounds with bronzed, muscular forearms and biceps. Black-haired and swarthy, noticeably taller than all the other fathers who stand around the picnic table supervising their children, he picks me up from my seat. He is able to hold me up with his forearm as I ogle the model plane.

Two years later when I was six, my father, who was then forty-one years old, was working at the top of a telephone pole. It was at the hottest arc of a summer day, and, as he later recounted it, he suddenly found himself falling, landing on his back in the middle of the street. An ambulance took him to an emergency room where he underwent numerous tests. Remarkably, he had no major injuries but remained in the hospital for two weeks.

The day after his accident, the doctors confided to us that he had had a mild stroke, but reassured us that there would be no lasting damage. But over the next couple of years we would realize they had been wrong. As it turned out, that moment on the telephone pole had been the first warning of severe hypertension, heart disease, and chronic anxiety that would rapidly worsen and plague my father for the rest of his relatively short life.

Before that happened, during his working days, in the early mornings he would put on too much Old Spice after-shave before heading to work. He would walk around and kiss my brother, my baby sister, Andrea, and me goodbye, the soles of his steel-toed climbing shoes squeaking on the wooden floor. I would always smell that cloying yet comforting scent as it lingered in the hall for a few hours after he left. But once he fell off the telephone pole, I would begin to associate him not with Old Spice, but with the permeating, sickening antiseptic smell of hospitals, the harsh industrial cleansers, the rancid smell of disease and of bodies heading rapidly toward death. Subsequently, whenever we came home from one of our visits to his hospital room, I would take long showers to scrub off that pervasive odor.

During most of these hospital stays, my father was assigned to a large ward with four or five other men. Usually, within a few days of entering the hospital, he would become the center of attention, the great raconteur, the good-time guy who flirted with the nurses and who made all of his buddies laugh. Often, when my mother would arrive for a visit with the three of us in tow, the guys in the ward would be cackling at something my father had just said. He would tell funny stories about old characters in his neighborhood, or about Miss Annie, the old gossip who lived around the corner from him, about all the nuts he encountered when he went to their houses to repair their telephones.

But as soon as he would see us in the doorway, his demeanor would change. His face would tighten as though ashamed he was having such a good time. He didn't want us to see him having fun. Then he'd solemnly pull the privacy curtain around us as we gathered around his bed. The guys in the ward would still be yelling from across the room that they could never recuperate with my father around because he kept them up all night laughing. "Hey, Buck," they'd call over to us, having learned his nickname, "open up that curtain and tell us another one." In many of his "ward stories," as the guys called them, my dad would recount the glory days of his youth when he was a star baseball player, and later on a scab buster and an amateur boxer. He had them cheering for his moments of victory. They asked for the vivid descriptions of injuries. Often when we were visiting him, a nurse would brusquely part the curtain to take his blood pressure. (When he was in the hospital, it was always a normal, healthy level.) With a sharp intake of breath, she'd shake her head in mock irritation. " Why do they even have you in here?" she'd say to him. "All you ever do is cut up and keep everybody else awake. They ought to send you home and give everybody else around here some peace and quiet." Privately, she would tell us how much fun it must be to have a father who was such a clown.

My brother, my sister and I would look at each other in bewilderment. Had we missed something? Had sickness and hospitals transformed our dad into a new man, lighthearted, quick to laugh, full of cheer and surprises, when we weren't around? There he became a bedridden impresario, orchestrating the day's entertainment for the ward and delighting everyone around him except his wife and three children when they came to visit several times each week.

Perched at his bedside in the hospital, I would be fascinated by all the machinery that whirred around him: the oxygen supplier, the heart monitor, the IV drip, the blood pressure reader. My six-year-old brain took inventory of all that was in this scene: my father, the big man, hooked up to all the life-monitoring equipment. I would think of the other fathers in the neighborhood whom he had maligned because of their height or their size, remembering how my father always claimed that a tall man, a broad man with physical presence was more of a "he-man" than one who was short or slight of build. He called diminutive men "pip-squeaks."

The moment my father left the hospital, he grew preoccupied and morose. He'd return home relaxed and supposedly stress-free. But within a few months, he slowly reentered his world of anxieties: money, health, a conviction that some household appliance would break, that the house would burn down or that we'd even be the victims of violent crime. He would try to control his restive turmoil with daily dosages of valium, but eventually he began taking so much that he developed a high tolerance to the drug and would have had to take almost lethal amounts to get the result he needed. Unfortunately, his doctors never controlled his Valium supply and his dependency wound up harming him more than it helped him.

Before his first illness, he had bought my brother and me boxing gloves and a punching bag, and built a basketball goal in the backyard. He'd taken us fishing and to see baseball games. He was a talented and meticulous carpenter who took pride in his property, modest as it was, and had taken on numerous home improvement projects.

He was still a massive man, but his posture had become stooped; he no longer stood proudly tall as he used to when he extolled the superior virtues of his height, which I would one day inherit. I saw how frightened he was of remaining sick, of maybe dying before his time. And I tried to imagine a moment when he could have fit the description of what he claimed to have been once. But as I looked at him I kept thinking of the fathers he had summarily dismissed, fathers who were still robust, still able to play with their children, to lift them up. The images of these other men, smaller, more thoughtful, began to replace my ideas of what a father should be and, slowly, they started to edge him out.

Indeed by the time my father was 45, he looked many years older. His facial expressions bloomed with worry, tension, and deep dissatisfaction, which often banded together to propel him full-speed into acute panic attacks. On other occasions, his bitterness came flowing out in diatribes about all that was wrong with the world.

I used to sneak looks at the photo albums from the days when he was on the aircraft carrier Hollandia. The pictures showed a surprisingly handsome young man laughing and proud to be standing on the flight deck in his navy uniform. And then there were the more recent pictures, taken when he was dating my mother, and the ones taken at our early birthday parties. I couldn't believe how old he had come to look in so short a time, how frail he now appeared. The deterioration of his health, the rapid, stark transformation it brought about in him in less than five years was staggering. I daydreamed of his being somehow restored to his youth, of once again walking down the streets late at night as other men moved aside to let him by.

At the same time that his heart began to beat erratically, his arteries began to harden, and the blood flowing to his brain slowed, causing dizzy spells and slurred speech. His underlying pessimism became much more pervasive, and he seemed determined to infect the rest of the family with it. His view of the world had not always been deeply pessimistic, my mother would tell me. It had just become that way in the years since he had fallen from the telephone pole. But now he began to lash out at us. He would tell us repeatedly, often with a menacing look on his face, "I don't give a damn if you like me. But you're gonna respect me and do what you're told if you know what's good for you." Veiled threats of beatings warned us not to step out of line. And yet Paul and I knew that in his state, there was little he could do to us. His rantings became more frequent as we entered adolescence, and I could only conclude that his angry and bitter threats were the only way he could feel he was imposing some control on his life.

To his credit, my father was not an acquisitive person and, outside of his always-modest cars, was not attached to material objects. But the one possession he did cherish was kept in the large metal fireproof box that contained many pieces of Navy memorabilia. It was a large picture frame, about two feet high, that he had made by welding together three 9 mm. gun shell casings that he had collected on his aircraft carrier. In the frame is a picture of him as a young enlisted man dressed in the navy blue uniform and white sailor cap: a man with thick dark eyebrows, the dark eyes of a prankster who would take pride in recounting his fighting conquests rather than his sexual ones – for he was also a man of many inhibitions. Indeed, he talked in hushed, embarrassed tones about the Hollandia's ports of call when his shipmates would go to whorehouses. He never did, he said, because he knew "it was a sin." He always told me these stories as though he were embarrassed about them, and his way of saying that one of his buddies had VD was that "the medic had to put his balls in a Bull Durham bag." He was embarrassed about things sexual, an attitude that dated back to his early adolescence when he came under the influence of his rigidly Catholic Uncle August, who was a rabid proselytizer.

In his hand-fashioned frame of gun shells, my father would eventually replace his own picture with one of my mother, taken when she was 25 and wearing a pink dress with a single strand of white pearls. It always seemed odd to me this portrait of a delicate, pretty, dark-haired woman dressed in pink and pearls—surrounded by shell casings. But my father saw it as a great homage to the beauty of my mother as well as to the might of America, his two passions as a young man. The frame represented for him his years as an adventurer, and he loved nothing more than to take it out to show my friends the dimensions of a shell casing, to demonstrate with his approximated sound effects how those huge guns and the even larger antiaircraft turret guns boomed as they were fired out over the ocean.

And so my father lived in the past. His constant reminiscences about those years in the Navy so many years before we were born always seemed such a sad preoccupation. It was because of this and his attitude toward his health that he became so self-absorbed that he never learned how to be the role model he desperately wanted to be.

Catherine's father, Hugh, was strapping, handsome, dignified, adventurous, widely read, well-traveled. He had been robbed once while buying emeralds in Bogota for his gem business in New Orleans. He loved to tell the story of fending off the crooks in an eerie, grimy South American back street. He still rode a motorcycle to his office, and had just begun studying for a pilot's license. He was the closest I had gotten in my seventeen sheltered, suburban years to what I thought was a true worldly figure.

I first met Hugh when Catherine invited me over to her house two years before she was raped. He was playing the guitar late at night, some classical Spanish piece. Twice the size of ours to accommodate their large family, Catherine's house was a Mediterranean-style white stucco house that her parents had built themselves. It wasn't grand by the standards of its architecture but was large and rambling and had real brick floors. It was filled with old family armoires and wing chairs, had bookshelves lined with leather-bound books, original oil and watercolor paintings, real silver flatware and ironed cloth napkins that were used for dinner every night.

Catherine, 17, was the youngest of eight children whose ages ranged up to 30. She had six brothers, all of whom were well-educated and naturally athletic. It seemed everyone in the family could discern good music, good art. Their bearing was that of the old Southern aristocracy, but they were comfortably well off rather than affluent. Their house was the first place in which I ever saw a copy of *The New Yorker*—not just one, but several back issues on a mahogany butler's table. Hugh, an avid reader, kept a subscription for years. He had a particular taste for the dog-and-messy-house cartoons of George Booth. In contrast to my father's demand for silence at the dinner table so he could watch Archie Bunker reruns (despite my mother's attempts to start meaningful conversation), the St. Clairs engaged in raucous dinner table discussions about politics, entrepreneurism, music.

Hugh liked to talk about keeping one's honor in the midst of trying to get a corner on the good life. He always said it was better to be your own boss, no matter what the risks were, than to become lost in a corporate maelstrom. My father, big as he was, tough as he claimed to be, was petrified of taking risks and was very much a company man. We didn't have many copies of magazines around the house. My father thought that having too many things, whether they were magazines or college degrees, was materialistic, for "heathens" and it meant that you valued things over God.

The night that I met Catherine's father, he was sitting up late, alone, strumming lightly on his guitar just as she had strummed on hers the night at the Butterfly. He was in the living room sitting against a high wall paneled with old doors made in another century, half in shadow created by the light of an antique pewter lamp. A half-filled glass of whiskey sat on a table next to him.

"This is Segovia" were the first words he ever said to me. "These chords are impossible." He extended his hand. He was leaning over from a battered old mahogany side chair whose seat was covered in dark green velvet. As we spoke, he continued to try to mold his fingers to the chords, trying to tune the guitar as he fiddled with the pegs to tighten the strings. "One of the most complex arrangers any musician will ever come across, but when some guy worth his salt plays him, that's when a serious guitarist really earns his dough."

Square-jawed, hair an even blend of blond and gray, he looked at us through square tortoise-shell professor glasses. He was wearing rumpled chinos and a Brooks Brothers Oxford shirt that wasn't tucked in.

Catherine and I had just returned from a repertory movie house where we had seen George Bernard Shaw's *Major Barbara*. When we told Hugh this he said, "Shaw had the clearest view of the importance of money. He came from a family without it and he was obsessed with how the wealthy had so many more choices in life. He could say it when no one else had been able to." Hugh turned to me. "There are two things you have to have in life and then everything else makes sense and will follow: love and money. If you have love and no money, you're always anxious. And if you have money and no love, you're always lonely and trying to figure out a way to get it. When you have the money, you think you are entitled to love, you think that it sets you up for being more lovable, so it makes it even worse when you have all the things you want, but not the one vital thing that you really need. When you have one without the other, you're always scheming for a way that you can get the one you don't have."

During this several-minute monologue, he continued to play very softly, stopping every few seconds to adjust the pegs. He laughed at himself. "When everybody else zigs, you should zag," he said to me in the trademark buttery tones of his upper-class Memphis accent. "I see you as a world traveler," he told Catherine, "with exotic tastes and exacting standards. One lover probably won't be enough for you. And you," he said to me, "maybe you'll live somewhere in the south of France and write books." When he drank, he gestured with his glass and his cigarette. Then he said that there were really only two tenets for living a good life: "we have to distinguish ourselves from the crowd, and we have to drink deep from the well. That's one of my favorite subjects for a sermon. Now you may all rise."

That night I remember lamenting how money shortages, over the years, had worn my parents down. They believed that having money would solve most of their problems, and that it would have made their lives happier. They were right. Although I had grown up just a few blocks away from Catherine, my house was part of a middle income tract housing community that had sprung up in the late 50s as New Orleans was suburbanized. There were four or five floorplans and brick colors, and they alternated up and down each street for block after block. It was a neighborhood made up primarily of young families who had come to our street until they could get on their feet financially and move on to a bigger house. We had stayed long past the time when most of our original neighbors had moved away.

HUGH'S LOVE-MONEY equation made brilliant sense to me because it gave me promise of a possibility that I never knew existed. And yet I realized that his vision of a good life was elegantly simple because he had never had to worry and would never have to worry, as we did, about how he was going to pay his monthly bills.

I told him this, and he immediately stopped playing the guitar and looked at me with surprise. He began to say something, perhaps it was an apology, something that would have been uncharacteristic for him because he was used to being listened to, used to being the family oracle that his wife and his children consulted. I had inadvertently challenged him. And because he knew that my life had been more difficult than that of his children, he suddenly seemed to regret his late-night grandiosity.

Hugh poured me another drink and began to ask questions. Personal questions about my parents, about what I hoped for in life. Catherine was in the room, but she soon fell asleep in the rocking chair.

And so I described my father and my mother and their families. I described growing up in a strong Catholic Cajun culture, a world made insular by the ethnic insistence upon speaking French. Not a pure Parisian French, but a patois that was augmented by many English words, many of which were Frenchified. I told him that my father, descended from a long line of alcoholics, was a black Irishman whose greatest pride was that he never succumbed to the vice that had undermined his native culture, not to mention the majority of men in his family who died of complications of alcoholism before they were sixty. I described my father's early labor union days when he beat up scabs, his fall from the telephone pole, his ongoing free fall into bad health. And after listening to me carefully, Hugh said, "And you think he's a failure?" I cringed when I heard this question, afraid of what my answer would be. The question angered me. By being honest, I felt I would betray my father. I was deeply conflicted. It was an ongoing struggle to reconcile how I saw him and who he was, and I didn't want anyone else to see him as I did. "I don't know," I said with shame.

"Don't mind me. I'm a pontificator," Hugh finally said, as though embarrassed about his prying question. "You have to be loud and quick and to the point in this family, because we all have a big opinion." So different from my own family, I thought, in which my father said the opinion of the "head of the house" should be the one "big opinion," despite my mother's overruling him every time.

In the coming months, Catherine would invite me to dinner and Hugh would draw me into family discussions about politics and social issues. I was an avid student of current events and politics and more liberal than he was. Nevertheless, he was eager to hear my opinions about the work ethic (he always said, "you don't work, you don't eat") and welfare—which he couldn't stand because he felt that people got something for nothing.

In fact, shortly after I met Hugh, the federal government created an assistance program in which families whose main breadwinners were disabled could apply at a food center for free staples such as cheese and milk and eggs. Sitting at the St. Clairs' dinner table, I was disturbed by the thought of my father thrilled by the idea of free food and, although we did not need public assistance, how he had stood for an hour in the cheese line at the food distribution center that had opened on the perimeter of a suburban housing project. Shortly after the center opened, a reporter from the metro desk of *The Times-Picayune* wrote a story about the new federal program, and my father made certain that he had his picture taken with a four-pound brick of yellow American cheese. His name was written in the caption below the photograph. My mother was mortified, because she was proud and had always worked very hard and deplored the idea of accepting welfare—to her, taking alms was out of the question, despite my father's growing sense of entitlement to it.

AROUND THE CORNER from the St. Clairs' house, down a bumpy, oak-shaded road a few blocks from the Mississippi River's west bank, lay an unused, two-acre parcel of land. The land belonged to a retired Navy captain known to everyone as The Chief, a man my father was in awe of from afar because of his distinguished Navy career. At the time, Hugh was high on the idea that people needed to learn how to become more self-sufficient. He dreamed up the notion of a community vegetable garden that could be shared by several families—including mine. He approached The Chief, who lived next door to the unused parcel, and told him that the soil was highly fertile and its productivity was being sadly wasted. Hugh was able to cajole the man into letting a selected few of us use the fallow ground to produce part of our food. He told The Chief that the garden would be a symbol of idealism and hope, a sign of what good people could bring about in their own lives if they just put their minds to it. My father, when he received Hugh's invitation (through me) to participate in the garden, was delighted with the idea of getting a break in the grocery bills.

The St. Clairs' plot was on the other side of ours, and that first morning I remember Catherine's mother was planting corn, laughing off the disagreements between my mother and Mary White over the virtues of organic gardening. "I'm just going to pretend I don't hear what they're saying," she chuckled. Mrs. St. Clair thought most confrontations were not only unpleasant but unnecessary. The archetype of a Southern lady, she shuddered in the face of discord, and instead of walking away from it, which would acknowledge the disagreement, she went about her business in the face of it and pretended it wasn't really happening. That day in the garden, she radiated maternal kindness in a lemon yellow sundress with a large sunflower on its front hip pocket. She was tall and trim, with a prominent thin nose and manicured, well-polished fingernails. Her waist-length hair was swept up into a bun as it had been every day from morning until night for the past thirty years. Everywhere she went, whether it was to a supermarket or to a garden party, Mrs. St. Clair wore a dress or a skirt and heels. Her bun was always intact.

My father was dressed in his typical uniform of baggy, knee-length, cut-off brown shorts, a white strapped undershirt, black, knee-high nylon support stockings, white sneakers, and a straw-brimmed hat. As he strung the poles for the pole-bean patch, his shoulders looked especially stooped and his spine, probably as a result of the fall, looked noticeably misaligned. Because he had already retired from the phone company on a disability pension, tending the garden would essentially become his new job. Over the next two years, until the Chief decided to accept a handsome offer for his vacant land, my father would spend more time alone there than anyone else. He would come to view the garden as his own turf, and felt intruded upon when too many other people showed up.

That first day Hugh finally showed up well after everyone else to see the project that he had originally conceived. It must have been his entrance that set my father off. Hugh arrived, just back from an early morning tennis game, dressed in his tennis whites. As he surveyed the scene of families raking and hoeing and planting, Hugh began to tell us that man should strive to be as self-sufficient as possible and how growing one's own food was fundamental to achieving that goal. Although I liked what he said, his lecturing sounded a bit absurd particularly because he delivered it in his tennis clothes. Nervously, I introduced him to my father, who warily shook his hand.

"Pleased to meet you, Buck," Hugh said, shaking my father's hand more vigorously.

The contrast between them was immediate and striking. Here were two men in their mid-50s, of the same age, the same height. But my father easily looked ten years older than Hugh. Particularly because of the way each was dressed, my father could have passed for Hugh's much older employee, the caretaker, and Hugh looked like the master, checking up on the day's work. "Looks like you have your work cut out for you," Hugh said as he watched my father stringing poles for the beans. Looking up and down our remaining rows that had not yet been tilled, Hugh said, "You're welcome to use the rototiller when we finish with it. It'll save you a helluva lot of work." He had rented a rototiller to make everyone's job much easier. My father, however, had already decided that using a rototiller was "a sign of materialism." And so struck the first discordant note of what would be their limited acquaintance.

"The trouble with the woil taday," my father began, "is they got too much materialism. People waste a lot of money on machines

39

that do the woik faster. Nobody woiks by hand no more. But woikin' by hand gives life meaning." And if this wasn't enough, my father, as was customary, followed with a non-sequitur. "People these days think too much about what they want next when what they oughta think more about is sayin' a prayer every now and then. All lem material things don't mean nuttin' to the Man Upstairs. What He's lookin' at is whether or not you praisin' Him and givin' glory to His name. When the rapture comes, he's comin' with it and He's gonna be mad as hell when he sees what's been happenin' to this woil."

After listening attentively to every word my father uttered, Hugh said, "You know, Buck, you may be right. But it's hard to believe in all of these things that you can't see. What if we're doing all this, not doing all the things we want to do just in case, and then in the end we find out we missed out on all the fun. Then," he laughed, "I'm going to be pretty pissed off."

My father looked up at him in exasperation. He had the same look on his face as the one I saw when I questioned him on something he felt was rhetorical. As he began to answer, his mouth twisted into what looked for a moment like an embittered smirk. His cheeks reddened with irritation. "You don't probably know about none of this stuff since you don't read the Bible. But that's all you need to know—what's in the big book. If it's in the Bible, that means Gawd said it and that's all I need to know about what I need to believe."

Again Hugh listened politely and attentively—I knew it was for my sake that he did so. But his face betrayed what he really thought of my father at that moment. He simply gave him a smile and a shrug, and as he leaned over to start the rototiller, said to my father, "Say a prayer for me, Buck. I could probably use one."

Later on that evening my father said about Hugh, "Typical college man. Thinks he's better than everybody else."

Although my father claimed to resent "college guys," when my brother and I went to college, he was deeply proud. There were other examples that showed how contradictory his thinking could be. Although he had tempered his use of racial epithets in my mother's presence and still professed a basic distrust of blacks, one time, during a flood, he offered a ride to a black woman and her three children whose car had stalled. He went so far as to bring them home to our house and insisted they use the phone to call for help.

At sixteen I was already ashamed of the man my father had become. But I was ashamed of him then because I was not yet smart enough to see that my father's earnest toil gave him virtue and that his teenage memories of his home life combined with his religious zeal had saved him from being a drunk. He had probably risen further from his origins than Hugh and many other men had risen from theirs. Given the family legacy he had inherited, Hugh had not had to move too far away from his family's origins and had preserved what he had acquired from a previous generation. My father had had to defy his family's legacies, and to try to create his own new guidelines, to survive.

My father made it clear to my brother and my sister that he favored me for my even temperament and physical resemblance to him. I was big for my age, taller than most other boys in my class. I had inherited his height and physique, and, I would later learn, some of his health problems. He beamed whenever someone recognized my resemblance to him and liked the fact that I looked like he once had. I embodied him, thus preserving what he'd lost. That physical resemblance was his most tangible connection to me, the only one that he could reach; any deeper bond, any emotional tie, was beyond his ability. In the end he relied too much on our physical resemblance; he felt it would guarantee a special relationship that he hadn't spent enough time trying to build.

Four

BECAUSE THE POLICE want to try to keep Catherine's identity a secret, it takes a few days for the incident of the rape and the capture to percolate down to the media. And at first none of us dare to tell anyone. Paul and I have been living in a rental apartment on Saint Charles Avenue and this is where the four of us retreat and recamp in a shell-shocked daze, particularly Catherine, who, we soon discover, is slipping even further away from us. From the moment Zachariah left us in the murky curtain of the river, from the moment Paul realized that we were saved from the treacherous currents, from the moment we began to wade back to shore, Catherine had begun to withdraw into her own cocoon where there was room inside only for her.

She tells us that when she first arrived at Charity Hospital, she expected to be whisked in to see an attending doctor. Instead, she was made to sit in a waiting room for what seemed like at least an hour, answering the routine questions of hospital attendants, many of whom could barely speak English. As she stood in front of the admitting desk, swaying on trembling knees and shaken from all that had happened in just the last couple of hours, she recited her social security number and gave other vital information. Standing there, she felt as though the hospital support staff couldn't have been less bothered to help her. By now it was the pre-dawn hours and the workers were clearly not interested in getting any work done. Finally a nurse brought her to an examining room. Woozy from lack of sleep, Catherine would always remember that the doctor who came to examine her was wearing a Rolling Stones T-shirt emblazoned with the cartoon image of Mick Jagger's big, wide-open mouth with its teeth parted and its long tongue sticking out in a mischievous, somewhat grotesque grin. She kept staring at the shirt because the image had always amused her, and she was trying to focus on it for diversion. At one point the doctor foolishly remarked that she seemed unusually calm after her ordeal and during such an invasive and traumatic exam; he even hazarded to say that he was surprised at how composed she appeared. This tore off the veil of numbness. Catherine suddenly became hysterical on the examining table and lay there screaming until she was finally comforted by the policewoman who had been waiting for her when she arrived at the hospital.

Once she calmed down she was given antibiotics and "morning after" pills. The antibiotics would reduce the possibility of her acquiring any sexually transmitted diseases and the "morning after" pills would start her period, thereby aborting any possible pregnancy. Finally, near daybreak, she was brought to the police department to give her statement and to make a positive identification of Zachariah Thomas in the police lineup.

CATHERINE ARRIVES at our apartment. Over several hours I notice a shift in her behavior. It isn't just that there's no knee-

44

buckling laughter, or sprightly behavior; she barely speaks, and stares vacantly ahead. She avoids direct eye contact, hardly eats or drinks anything. She gives weak, half-thought responses to our elementary questions regarding how she's doing and if we can do anything for her. And when we dote too much, she feebly waves us off. It's as though all of her vital energy has been sucked out by Zachariah Thomas, or worse still that her whole body still reels from his assault, all her waking thoughts unwittingly trained on the violence of what he did to her, reliving it moment by moment, emotion by emotion, sensation by sensation. This terrifies me. Clearly she needs to be seen by a professional, but at any mention of the idea she shakes her head vehemently as she stretches her fingers into claws and digs into wherever she happens to be sitting or standing.

The only subject that could provoke any kind of sustained response is when she's going to tell her parents, which she refuses to do. Every time I bring it up, she snaps into a personality that I've never seen before. She becomes darkly serious, adamant, as she exclaims that she would never let her family know. Part of her refusal, I will come to realize, is a protective instinct towards us, her friends. She knows her father and her six brothers will go crazy when they hear she was raped, and without a way to vent their outrage she fears they'll train it on Paul and me and Alex. We're acutely aware of this. We're afraid of it, too, but we also know that our families have to be told, that what has happened is too complex and appalling for us to deal with it on our own. Particularly for Catherine, who is at the time unemployed and clearly needs counseling, which cannot be given without her parents' involvement.

She manages to call home and say that she's staying with us— with me. And since Hugh trusts me, they have no problem with this. I listen to her phone calls to her mother, and how she manages to make herself sound pert and upbeat, but I can see it summons all of Catherine's reserves to sound normal. But the moment she gets off the phone, she begins a long and rapid slide into an inconsolable depression.

The weekend passes. I somehow go back to my job of selling shoes and taking my last semester of classes before going abroad. Paul returns to work at a hotel in the French Quarter, continuing his leave of absence from college. Catherine, who is a full-time student, forces herself to go back to class. We all confess to having difficulty concentrating at work, to begin our lives again. We watch Alex standing in front of the mirror, coming his hair into a ducktail, checking his appearance from every angle, before taking to the streets to resume his evening trade. Although he hangs close to us here at the apartment, he stands apart because he escaped before the worst of it began. It's clear to the rest of us that he's already bounced back, his body still perfect and unmarked and commanding the high prices from his Johns. The many confrontations with life on the streets of New Orleans have given him good preparation for a time like this. The rest of us are raw and sore, we are already inhabiting a different reality. Paul has a hematoma on his right leg from being kicked by Zachariah Thomas. I'm covered with sickly yellow bruises and my groin still aches, and like my brother, my thoughts are hazy and disconnected. Catherine has dark fingermarks on her throat.

At night, Catherine and I are often alone together, but sadly each in our own separate worlds, so that we rarely *are* together when we are in the same room. Time is moving by painfully slowly, as it does when you're too sick to get out of bed. I want to speed it up, for days to accumulate because only time will allow the chemistry of our minds and bodies to revert back to normal. And so, to keep myself steady I dream of what my life will be like in the amber light of Rome.

Finally the television station where Catherine's father worked reports the story, a skeletal account of what has happened, no names mentioned in a brief sketch of a crime and capture. The racial element is introduced as a matter of course. Sitting there, listening to the incident being reported by Angela Hill, a locally famous bleach-blonde news anchor, I imagine that, in the coming days as more details of the story leak, Marla Boudreaux's Dixie beer story will be played to the hilt, and she'll be shown outside her shotgun house, wearing a different version of the same outfit—a lime green tube top and kahki jeans with her own embroidery—regaling reporters with her blow by blow description of everything she saw. And I imagine Angela Hill, about whom Clo, my nasty grandmother, once said, "You can tell that when she gets off television and goes home at night she smells herself," praising Marla Boudreaux's ability to outwit her assailant. I sit there thinking how all of this would belittle my brother and myself. I look over at Catherine, whose head is dropped to her chest as though she's nodded out. But I know she's awake. I know she's listening to Angela Hill.

I'm about to tell Catherine that now that the news has broken it will be only a matter of time before her parents will find out that she is the victim of a rape and that she must tell them herself and not let them find out from anyone else. But the phone rings. It's my father calling me to make sure that I know Anwar Sadat, the president of Egypt, has been assassinated in his own country. "Oh and by the way," he says, "a group of college students" had been attacked in Audubon Park. No names were used in any of the articles, he says, but did I happen to know who they were because some of them were thought to be students at the university where Catherine and I were in school.

I'm thoughtfully silent for only a split second and then I say, "Yeah, I know who they are."

"Who were they?" says my father. "Who?"

The eyes of Paul and Catherine and Alex are on me. I know that Paul wants me to tell the truth. Whether or not I tell the truth hardly matters to Alex, who doesn't have a family. Catherine is the only one who is looking at me and resolutely shaking her head.

"Yeah, dad. It was us."

He is silent on the other line.

"You can't tell anybody, okay. I need . . ."

The phone line dies away.

Numbed, I hang up. Catherine bursts into tears.

The phone rings again a few minutes later, and I answer it. This time it's my mother, sounding breathless. "What is going on, Barry, please tell me." My father, she explains, has just taken a Valium.

We were the crime victims, I tell her, and she reacts by saying, "Oh no, no," as though it is still going on and she's trying in vain to say that it hasn't happened. Then I say we will come home immediately to talk about it.

Paul and I leave Catherine with Alex and drive to our parents' house. It is a sullen drive past the darkened old mansions lining Saint Charles Avenue, and then along the dilapidated wharves of Tchoupitoulas Street. We edge the waterfront and file onto the metal span of the Mississippi River Bridge that connects the French Quarter and the Garden Districts with the suburbs on the West Bank, where many people, including my parents, fled the increasingly crime-ridden, honky tonk streets of the French Quarter with its topless bars and sidewalk Martini stands and the eerie, mugger-filled streets of the adjacent Faubourg Marigny neighborhood.

As we fly across the bridge, I look through the interstices of girders down at the river, not far from where I was nearly forcibly drowned the night before, and I think to myself I never would have imagined that things would get even worse, that there would be consequences to face for what had happened, as though I had done something wrong. The strange, appalling vision of Zachariah Thomas driving in his Cordoba rises up, his face impassive, his derisive laughter echoing in the parking lot. And then Angela Hill's brief summation of the crime, thirty seconds of airplay describing an incident that most people would listen to and then discard as one more crime statistic, the complications of which they'd never realize. It's inconceivable that so many of these incidents go on every day all over the country.

When we walk in the door of my parents house, the curtains are drawn and there is darkness, but this is not in any way unusual. My parents keep them like this all the time whenever the weather is stifling. My mother's eyes are sensitive to the sun, and my dad reasons that if the sun shines in the windows, it will heat up the house and raise the electricity bills from the air conditioning. My mother waits for us in the living room that my father and my brother jointly built as an addition to the existing structure of the house. She looks pale and grave as she sits in a corduroy La-Z-Boy recliner, pensively staring into space. The moment we breeze in the door, she cantilevers herself until her feet touch the ground. But she doesn't get up. She sits there, gripping the arm rests. "Look at you two. Just look at you," she exclaims, as she notices the scratches and bruises on us.

"Where's Dad?" Paul says.

"He's in the bedroom lying down." My mother rolls her dark eyes. "He can't handle this."

My mother is forty-eight years old, with parchment pale skin that, due to her aversion to the sun, is without a splotch or a wrinkle. Her skin is as fine and as delicate as lace. Her eyes are dark and hooded and have a natural cast of what I'd call shrewd suspicion. They also let on that she knows more about people and the vagaries of human nature than she needs to be told. She is deeply shy.

But in the past several years, in the face of my father's illness, she has come to be seen in our extended family, and certainly to her three children, as a heroine who had been forced to take on several difficult roles as leader of the family. She has had to return to work, to manage all the finances, to find money for three private schools, to make all important household decisions and to raise us as a single parent, not to mention oversee my father's many medical and psychological needs. These challenges have been monumental for a deeply Catholic Southern woman, taught to be subservient to her husband, taught to mistrust nearly any independent thought she would ever have that did not agree with the narrowly defined view of the world that her family, the Church, and the community have always said was defined by the gospel. Out of necessity, she has risen far above the limitations of these edicts.

"So tell me what happened. I just want to hear it from the beginning," she says. She listens, wincing. But when we tell her that Catherine was raped at gunpoint and how Zachariah Thomas behaved as though to degrade us, the color drains from her face and then rises again as her shock surfaces, ebbs and then reemerges as anger. And yet, as angry as she gets, she makes no racial slur, for this would go against her grain. Like my father's parents, her parents were also racist, and part of her being able to survive the legacy of their poor judgment and education was to show compassion and understanding of racial differences. She also knows that my father will tred heavily on race issues, and perhaps is already bracing herself to do battle with him.

"Now I can understand why Catherine doesn't want to tell Hugh," my mother says eventually, her way of giving vent to the troublesome issue.

"She's got to," Paul says. "Somebody else will if she doesn't."

"Oh, I know. I know."

"Look at this," Paul says and lowers his trousers a discreet amount to show her his raging hematoma.

"Barry, you okay?" she asks, coming over to me and brushing me across the shoulders."

"I wish I could wind the time back," I tell her.

And then she says that as bad as we feel, Catherine must feel worse. Because the rape puts the crime and its repercussions in a whole different category. She says that if anything like that had happened to our sister, hearing it, knowing it would make my mother want to jump out of her skin.

"Is Catherine at your place now? Will she answer the phone?" Mom asks.

We shrug.

"Well then let me call her."

We expect our mother to pick up the telephone right in front of us in the living room, but instead she walks down the short hall to my sister's bedroom and uses the phone in there. She doesn't want us to hear what she has to stay.

My mother and Catherine stay on the phone for a half hour and then my mother comes out of the closed bedroom, her brow furrowed, looking more troubled than before. "She can't do it. She just can't. I understand."

She quickly replays the gist of the conversation, how she told Catherine that though it might be difficult now, she had to try to keep in mind how she was going to feel in the future when she'd have terrible flashbacks to that night and would need her parents to be able to listen and understand. The problem, my mother had pointed out, was if Catherine were to withhold the information, they would find out eventually—they'd have to—and would always feel that their daughter had cut them out of the most devastating thing that had ever happened to her—and perhaps to them, too. My mother's words had impact.

"They just won't understand how it happened," Catherine apparently had said, crying over the phone. "Mom might. Dad won't."

Now, my mom takes a deep, nervous breath. "So I told Catherine that your father and I would go over there and tell them. And that once we did she should just go home herself."

"And she agreed?" I ask quickly.

My mom nods her head.

"So when are you going to do this?" Paul asks.

My mother motions toward the back of the house where our father lies nearly comatose on Valium. "As soon as he snaps out of it, I suppose. But they've got to be told right away."

Paul and I hang around the house. My mom unfreezes some crab gumbo and makes some rice. We all have a glass of iced tea. My brother and I feel a little better now, knowing that someone else is taking some of the burden off our shoulders. Eventually our sister, Andrea, comes home and is told. She's only 14 and although she's rather street smart and understands about such sexual crimes, she gets overwhelmed by what has happened. And then she says it's terrible that the responsibility has fallen on my parents to tell Catherine's parents. She says what Paul and I each are thinking but have not said ourselves. Andrea, the most outspoken member of the family, is unafraid to utter truths even when they are painful. More than once she's told my father what she thinks of him.

Finally, we hear stirrings in back of the house, and my father shuffles out into the shuttered house, unshaven and in a loose-fitting pair of shorts and a strapped undershirt. At first he won't even look at us. And when he does, he acts like he's been the victim of the crime. "How we gonna live this one down?" he agonizes. "This is a real mess." He sits in the La-Z-Boy recliner and starts wringing his huge, gnarled hands.

"We have to go over to the St. Clairs' and tell them what happened," my mother finally tells him.

His unshaven jaw drops open.

"You heard me. We have to tell them."

"It's not our responsibility," he mutters.

"She can't tell them. She feels that she's unable to. I understand."

"It's not our business," my father says. He glances warily at me and tssks. "I ain't gonna get involved in this."

"Well, then I'll tell them," my mother concedes.

"It's not your business, either!" my father keeps insisting.

"Never mind that. I'm going over there as soon as you can get dressed. Because you're coming with me."

"I'm not goin' nowhere."

"Yes, you are," my mother insists fiercely. "You will drive with me over to the St. Clairs'. You can stay in the car if you want while I go inside, but you have to drive me over there."

So, he can't face Hugh with this news, I think. I assume that my father will refuse to even get in the car and wait for my mother. But he surprises me. He actually drives her the half mile to the St. Clairs'.

He has to simply because my mother has never learned to drive. During the fifties, my father had tried to teach her, but grew impatient and told her she had no ability for steering a car. She has lived all these years in the suburbs and has had to depend on him to take her wherever she needs to go.

Paul and Andrea and I sit quietly after my parents leave. I think to myself that what my mother is about to do is an act of bravery, particularly for someone as socially shy as she is. It will take me years to get the whole story of what is said at the St. Clairs', but this, as much as I can ever know, is what happened.

My father drives my mother to the St. Clairs' house, parks the car in front, doesn't even bother to pull in the driveway. My mother gets out, dodges the trunk of a massive oak tree whose roots buckle the concrete, and walks up a brick path to the front door. She rings the bell and is answered by Catherine's mother who is holding a needlepoint canvas on which she has been stitching an intricate, tiny stitch of brightly colored yarn. The two women know one another only from the garden; they are friendly but not friends, each aware that they inhabit different social worlds. And although she is a model of politeness, Catherine's mother looks seriously puzzled to see my mother standing there, flushed and nervous. "What is it?" she asks rashly before her better instincts kick in and she invites my mother into her house. "Something's happened, hasn't it?"

My mother, no doubt glad to begin unburdening herself says, "Yes, something has happened. I don't know if you heard that a group of kids were attacked in Audubon Park two days ago, but Paul and Barry and Catherine were among them."

Mrs. St. Clair's face shrivels against the news. It doesn't make sense to her, because, "I've talked to Catherine several times in the last few days. She didn't say anything about it."

My mother barrels on. "Nobody has been . . . badly hurt. They got the man who did it. He's been arrested. But, well, there's more to it. I need to talk to both of you about it."

In her own retelling of the story, my mother says that this is the worst part, because as a parent you suddenly know something is terribly wrong, something is going to be told to you about your child's well-being that you don't want to hear and know you have to. According to her, a lot of being a parent is having to hear bad news about your children that will tear you apart more than any bad news that you've ever heard about yourself. You have this roaring instinct to protect and shelter what you've shepherded into this world, and it never goes away, even when your children grow up, just as I suppose, the feeling never goes away that you are somebody's child and that you must answer to your parents until they die.

And so, knowing that she will give Catherine's distressing news, my mother somehow finds the resources of compassion to take control of a situation that she would normally shy away from. And perhaps several years from then when Mrs. St. Clair will call my mother after she learns that my sister Andrea has cancer, there will once again be a similar moment of silent suffering between two mothers who might offer one another comfort regardless of the social gap that exists between them.

"Where is Hugh?" my mother says. "Let's go sit down and talk to him about it."

My mother follows Mrs. St. Clair past the dining room, where a long, antique cherry-wood dining table seats ten, a place where I have often sat listening to heated political discussions that were to me like holy cant, past cases of leather-bound books, past breakfronts holding precious heirloom crystal, past a circular mahogany liquor cabinet attached to a wall. They move into an adjacent living room filled with nineteenth-century tables and chairs that sit on red Spanish tile floors that are padded with Turkish kilem rugs. Hugh is sitting in the living room, dressed in tennis whites. He is holding a piece of polished gray stone, rolling it around in the palms of his hands as he flicks the TV's remote control through the late afternoon lineup of news shows and a tennis match, which finally stays on the screen. My mother is hearing the thwock of tennis balls being pounded back and forth as she says, "I'm sorry to barge in on your Sunday. But I have something to tell you."

The something is clearly unpleasant and monumental enough to bring my mother to a house where she has never been. And yet, Hugh does not turn off the tennis match, and for a moment my mother is distracted by the sounds of the sport and the applause that crackles as the result of a winning point. She even notices that Hugh lets his eye momentarily drift back to the screen.

Mrs. St. Clair tells her husband what my mother told her. He looks concerned, but it doesn't get to him as my mother might think. Perhaps he's automatically minimizing the kind of danger his daughter might have been in. Finally he stops rubbing the stone between his hands and once again fixes his eyes on my mother.

"The kids were attacked and robbed," my mother says. "But the guy who attacked and robbed them also . . . raped Catherine *at gunpoint*." The words just give birth to themselves. Now sitting down, Mrs. St. Clair throws her hands up to her face, letting the needlepoint canvas drop to the floor. Hugh takes the news in for a moment, his body crumpling. Then he throws the stone in his hands hard across the room. It ricochets off the floor, bounces against a window and breaks through cleanly like a bullet would. "Goddamnit!" he screams. "How many guys were there with her?"

"Three," my mother tells him.

"Three?" He slams his fist down onto the top of a table. Mrs. St. Clair reaches for a cigarette with a trembling hand. "Three guys couldn't take on one nigga?" There, the word is said and my mother has been expecting it, and although she has refused to use it herself, she would never admonish Hugh for doing so.

"What kind of men are they?" he yells at my mother. Mrs. St. Clair lights her cigarette.

"He was holding a loaded, cocked gun to her head the whole time," my mother says.

Mrs. St. Clair quietly agonizes, "But why didn't she tell us? Does she think we wouldn't understand, or that we wouldn't be able to help? It seems to me we should have been the first ones to know."

My mother says that Catherine was petrified of their reaction and that they would blame her for some kind of irresponsible behavior.

"How could we do that?" Mrs. St. Clair cries out.

Hugh has grown silent, his neck muscles straining, his face completely red. He's trying to restrain himself, all his good breeding bidding him to do so. He speaks again, his voice somewhat modulated, "She was with *three* men. How could one . . . get it over on all of them?"

Precisely, I would think when I heard this. And who knew what Hugh would say when he found out some boozy slattern coldcocked Zachariah Thomas. I know these ironies were the reason my father refused to face Catherine's father. Amazingly, however, my mother has a comeback. She stands up imperiously, facing Hugh and says, "Their lives were at stake and they were all trying to think what they could do to save each other. Barry stood up to him when he first tried to touch her. But the man kicked him where it hurts and told him he'd kill him. And Catherine said she was afraid that he would kill them. And that's why she didn't try to fight."

"Why didn't she tell *us?*" implores Mrs. St. Clair, no doubt mortified that my mother has had intimate information about her daughter before she did herself.

"They're all alive, Hugh," my mother intones. "I know it might not be a consolation now, but it will be. And the policemen who came there told them that they had done the right thing."

But this has no affect on Hugh, who shakes his head and says, "No, they could've done something."

MY MOTHER returns home calmer than she left, and when we ask her how it went at the St. Clairs' she says it could've gone worse. We ask her to tell us Hugh's reaction and she says his reaction was "what one would expect" and we don't press any farther. The important thing is that they know. My mother goes into Andrea's room to call Catherine at our apartment and tell her to go home. But the line is busy. And then there is no answer at our apartment.

The next day Catherine's mother calls to say that no one in their family blames anyone, and that the last thing they want to do is cause more trouble for us. Catherine's sister flies in from

Houston and she and Catherine come to visit Paul and me, bringing bottles of rootbeer and vanilla ice cream. But I know to stay away from her father. With a lingering sense of shame that I could have done more to protect her, I feel resentful that he expected me to have had control over an uncontrollable set of circumstances. And yet I also know that it's logical for him to blame me, since, that night at Audubon Park, I had been responsible for protecting his daughter.

AS THE DAYS finally begin to accumulate, and I get some distance on the event, I realize that I am now more acutely aware of the chances for random acts of violence, of the signs of potential danger that I had never noticed before. When I stroll through the French Quarter or near my apartment uptown, I do so with a chip on my shoulder, my temper wound tight around a short fuse. I'm ready to spring on the first person who seems remotely threatening. The most insignificant sounds make me edgy, provoke rage at what I think might be a mugger walking behind me but what ends up being a tree branch rustling in the wind or a cat cutting its way along a high wall. I create elaborate fantasies of revenge. A guy walks up behind me, pulls a gun, and tells me he wants to rob me. I comply, but as he continues to wave the gun in my face, I jump him, knock the gun out of his hand, and pound his head and face until he is bloody and senseless and unrecognizable. Someone pulls me off of him before I realize he's dead. And when I retell the story and catalogue his injuries, I tell them in detail, with gory descriptions of how I have beaten him beyond recognition—his eyes swollen shut, his face one massive hematoma, his lips split on the few teeth that remain in his mouth.

And I imagine my father in his pugnacious youth prowling the streets "lookin' for trouble" starting a fight with an unsuspecting stranger who happens to be in a bar or walking down the wrong street at the wrong moment. These fantasies will abate with time, but before they do, I am surprised by the dangerous growling current of my own hostility toward no one in particular. And I wonder if my search for what I need to prove about myself is as urgent as my father's had once been. For I finally see the primal compulsion that made it necessary for him to see himself as a conqueror. He had always felt he lacked control, especially when his embittered mother drove him out into the night to bring his father back from some local alcoholic shame. Was she asking "what kind of man are you?" when, on one of his many patrols, he had failed to find my grandfather?

Five

SEVERAL WEEKS LATER, we are summoned to the District Attorney's office to once again give individual statements about what happened. We are called in together but, after we arrive, Maria Rossi, one of the young assistant DAs, ushers us into an office one by one. First she spends an hour and a half with Catherine, then an hour with Paul. Maria tells Paul that with several different parties involved and the fact that the case is already drawing media attention (even though our names have not been used) there are many ways for the statements and future testimonies to go awry.

My turn to be questioned finally arrives. I am ushered into a cramped empty office enclosed by thick glass and Venetian blinds, the space barely large enough to contain a metal desk and a few chairs. I hear someone clipping down the hallway in heels. Maria breezes into the office, arms laden with manila legal folders and an empty coffee mug. She dumps her load of papers onto her desk and holding the cup up asks, "Want some?" I shake my head. She throws herself with a flourish into her high-backed black swivel desk chair. Maria wears her chestnut brown hair long, down to her hips. It sways from side to side as she moves, shimmering when she laughs her deep, throaty laugh. She is dressed entirely in black. More often than not she wears black, and I will learn that her colleagues have nicknamed her Contessa Negra.

"So, what we want to do here is to go minute by minute through everything you remember happening that night in as much detail as you can recall. It doesn't matter how insignificant it may seem to you, just say whatever comes to your mind. But try to think about this chronologically from the time you left home until the police came." She's fast-talking and speaks with a gravelly voice in the accent of her native north Louisiana.

Facing me directly, she says, "Details, details, details. Of everything that happened. Of everything that occurred to you while it was happening. Of every step you took. I have copies of the police report here in front of me. Statements that the police took from each of you individually. I'm using them as a guide to make sure what was originally taken down jives with what you tell me." I must look quizzical because she elaborates, "Sometimes these statements can have inaccuracies in them, especially when a victim is reporting a crime to the police for the first time. So don't go crazy if we find that something's wrong and we have to make sure later that everything you tell us is accurate."

Of course we would not be allowed to see or hear what each of the others had said.

"So," Maria says, staring at me and twirling a pencil, "tell me what happened from the beginning."

And so I retell the story, as I had several times already, but this rendition has more details. I tell her about the sound of Catherine's guitar, the lull we had fallen into, the sense of unreality that descended on us as we saw Zachariah approaching from a distance, his floating walk that clues us in that he's high on something, the fact that even though individually we were all nervous about his approaching, we sat there and did nothing. None of us wanted to admit that we were made more nervous by the sight of a scraggly black person approaching us than we would by a white person dressed similarly. Each of us—except for Alex—felt as though we had to have a more beneficent attitude toward minorities. After all, we had grown up in a racially divided city that smoldered with anger, perhaps not as much as other places, but nevertheless a palpable anger. We wanted to think of ourselves as more enlightened, more progressive than our parents, moving farther away from archaic notions of race and class that exist in so many American cities, especially in the South. If we became so alarmed at the sight of a disheveled black man, so alarmed that we rose up and fled, wouldn't that be proving our innate prejudice?

Of course, once Zachariah began brutalizing us, these concerns flew out the window, and all we wanted to do was survive the ordeal. Several times during my monologue, Maria mutters under her breath. The descriptions, particularly of the rape, appear to affect her more than I would have imagined. Is it the way I am telling the story, or just the fact that this seemingly tough, street savvy woman has more strands of sympathy running through her than I would have thought?

"That must've been hell for you, to watch that happening and be unable to stop it." Maria glances at me solemnly, but then her eyes dart down to her notes. She begins to say something else, but then holds herself in check. And then it dawns on me that she is casting for a way to say something tactfully. "I asked Catherine about your relationship." I visibly stiffen and Maria waves her hands at me. "I have to ask about all the relationships because it will come up at the trial, when the jury is hearing evidence. In fact, there will be many questions asked that will make you un-comfortable so you may as well get used to it now."

I say nothing. I don't want to discuss my aborted, unsuccess-ful relationship with Catherine. We were not sexually compati-ble, and it took me a long time to accept that. It did not diminish our friendship and certainly it didn't make me feel any less re-sponsible for protecting her.

"Have you two been sexually involved recently?" Maria asks softly.

"No. But why do you have to know this?" My impatience and anger are rising.

"The other side is going to want to know. They may—they probably will—try and suggest that she was being seductive. "

"That's crazy."

"Well . . . crazy or not, she told me that she acted as though she was enjoying herself, as a way of trying to make sure that he did-n't hurt any of you more than he did. She kept her head. I admire her for that. Unfortunately, this can and perhaps will be miscon-strued. As some kind of solicitation. A bunch of kids drinking wine get out of hand and go to some isolated spot in Audubon Park to have a gang bang and invite a stranger, who happens to be black, to join in. To participate. As a kind of novelty. A sideshow."

"That's insane!" I protest.

"Well, so are many legal arguments," Maria points out. Hesi-tating a moment, she says, "Besides, according to Catherine, as the gun was pointed at her, she and Zachariah had a discussion about what she was going to do with him and if she ever had a black man before. Were you aware of this?"

I nod my head. "But what does that mean? Will he try to say that it was something she wanted?"

"As I said, he may, but we have evidence of him forcing her. Bruises, the guns, and, of course, your testimony. Now what about the gun she had. Did you know she had it?"

I shake my head. I catch Maria's glance. "If I did know . . ." I begin. "Things would've been different."

"How?" Maria asks.

"I would've shot him," I said. "I would've killed him."

Maria looks doubtful and chuckles. "I hope you're not asked this question in court."

"Why?" I say. "It would only be self-defense?"

Now, do you know why she had a gun in her purse?"

I never knew that Catherine's father had given guns to both her and her mother and taught them how to shoot. In the small retail business he owned, Hugh had had to deal with thieves and numerous break-ins when the store was closed and had come to believe that his luck would one day run out. He kept several guns in the house and made sure family members knew how to use them. And yet I had no idea that Catherine carried a gun. She will confess later on that she had been taught to shoot to kill.

The conversation goes on: more questions, more answers, for what seems like hours but only ends up being perhaps thirty minutes more. Finally, we get to the nightmarish appearance of the tan Chrysler Cordoba, and how Paul and I first thought it was somebody who could help us. And how when we all moved into the path of the oncoming car we were determined to stop the driver to ask for help, and when we saw it was him, Zachariah, it seemed like a cruel joke was being played on us.

"And you're sure it was him," Maria asks.

"Positive. He looked right at us."

"How did he look at you?"

I explain that, actually, he looked right through us, as though it didn't even register with him that we were there.

"Well then perhaps one could say that he looked at you as though he didn't recognize you."

Not realizing she is playing devil's advocate, I say, "But I thought the police found his car a few hours later and it matched the description we gave of the tan Chrysler."

"They found a set of keys on the suspect. They were keys to a Chrysler car. They took the keys and combed the neighborhood, and they found a Chrysler Cordoba and the keys fit the lock."

"And it was tan, right?"

"It was, but I'm trying to get further evidence from all of you to substantiate that."

And then I remember something that I didn't remember before. And I suppose this is what Maria had been speaking about at the beginning of the interview. That certain things would be remembered differently over time, in each successive recollection, and remembering them differently wouldn't necessarily mean that I was imagining them. But suddenly, my mind's eye spots something in the car, something on the dashboard, illuminated, reflected, iridescent in the street lamps that had just come on in the parking area. A green and white package of Kool cigarettes. Maria's face lights up when I tell her this. She explains that when the police apprehended Zachariah at Marla Boudreaux's, and after they combed the neighborhood with his keys looking for a car they would fit, they found, among the other pieces of evidence, a green and white pack of Kools on the dashboard. Shortly after this revelation, my interview ends.

OVER THE NEXT few weeks and months, our lives slowly drift back to their normal routines. The only real difference is that I now avoid going to Catherine's house as a way of skirting a direct and prolonged confrontation with her father. But then I resent my own determination to evade him. For I know that I just can't leave things as they are, that at some point I will have to bridge the differences between us. I also know that the longer I remain quiet, the longer I avoid what is essential—confronting what I dread more than anything else—the more I may appear to be responsible for what happened. I'm struggling to move forward, to go on with life, to stop feeling like I've been a victim. It's not easy.

Almost immediately after the incident, Catherine starts seeing a psychiatrist. It's Hugh's idea. He does his homework, finds his daughter somebody who has dealt with the sort of trauma she has been through. Years later Catherine will tell me that Hugh introduced the idea of seeing a therapist by explaining that she would have nothing to be embarrassed about because this particular woman had heard everything in her line of work. And that talking to someone to whom you pay a lot of money protects the transference that happens in the analysis by keeping it on a business level.

Catherine spends many sessions replying to simple questions such as "How are you?" and "What do you think about what happened?" These are enough to set her off weeping and wailing. At first she consciously remembers trying to dam out the flood of guilt and remorse she felt at being in a potentially dangerous place after dark and then having to bear the shame of being the victim of a sexual crime that becomes public knowledge. But then of course these feelings seep out and are hashed and rehashed. What happens next, she will explain, is a sudden hyperawareness of the social and psychological differences between people. She's never before realized that there are people living in the world with no sense of morality, no conscience and that they reach these depths as the result of having been completely alienated. According to Catherine, many rape victims such as herself have such a hard time understanding how somebody could choose them. Instead of trying to understand that there is a personal history that led up to the moment of their being attacked, they find it easier to take the attack personally.

Like me, Catherine is plagued with fantasies, but hers are not so much of revenge but rather of being attacked again. Weeks, months, even years after the event, she will be out at night and suddenly find herself in a paralysis of panic.

IN THE SPRING Paul returns to school, and when he goes back, Alex also decides to leave town. He calls Paul to report that he is living in rural Louisiana as the houseboy to an esteemed New Orleans doctor. The doctor has promised to pay for Alex's college tuition and will help pave the way for a legitimate career. Whether or not he has finally gone "legit," he is the most difficult one of us to contact, and his protracted absences from New Orleans end up annoying the district attorneys who, trying to build their case, need to question and requestion him about various issues.

Alex has never been close to me, but he finally calls me late one night, because he can't find Paul in New York.

"Paul has moved," I explain. "He didn't know how to get ahold of you to let you know."

"Is he coming back for the summer?" Alex asks.

"He's not sure. He probably will. Because they say the case may go to trial in the summer. Either that or September."

"What about you. You gonna be around?

I tell him I'm supposed to leave for Europe in July.

The time has now come for me to buy my plane ticket—a supersaver—and with trepidation, I call Maria Rossi. "Don't worry," she reassures me. "I don't think it's gonna get started for a while. But you may have to come back to testify. We'll be liable for any ticket changes you have to make."

And yet I have a psychological block against having to interrupt my journey. I'm afraid that it will symbolize being held back from my life in some way, and I'm determined to leave New Orleans without any obstruction. To ward off this sense of accumulating uncertainty, I finally gather my necessary documents. Riding the fifteen-speed Fuji that I'd saved for and bought—with the help of my mother—for life in Italy, I cycle over to the International Trade Mart, on the east bank of the Mississippi, downtown, to apply for my passport.

I wind my new bicycle with chains and attach them to a heavy-duty lock and go inside to the passport agency only to be met with long, snaking lines of bedraggled-looking people. It takes me forty-five minutes to reach the passport window, and all the time I'm worrying that my bicycle will be stolen by one of New Orleans' marauding professional bicycle thieves. I'm anxious as I exit the building, straining my eyes to see if my maroon Fuji is still at the bicycle rack. And the moment I recognize it, glinting in the powerful sunlight, I notice Hugh St. Clair walking toward me.

There is no way we can avoid each other. I wave to him and at first he seems completely at ease and relaxed to see me. He has come to renew his passport for a trip to France that he will be taking to buy antiques which he will ship back to New Orleans and sell at a good profit to Louisiana Francophiles. He is dressed in a seersucker suit. He takes a brochure out of his briefcase and shows me offerings of a gallery that he does business with in France. With great enthusiasm he points out one piece in particular, an ornate armoire that is six feet tall and which he can purchase for an incredibly low price.

It occurs to me that even as I had once looked up to Hugh, he, too, in some way, maybe had pinned hopes on me, hopes that I'd one day live out some fantasy that he would have had for himself at my age, a fantasy of adventure, of bettering myself and ultimately transcending my background. Now things had turned out very different. Even though I was getting set to be on my way to Europe, following a trajectory that I had listened to him set for his own children, I assumed that he must see me as part of the defiling of his daughter. Our street friend, Alex, had chosen the spot that night, he knew about it and we had had to say it when we were asked the inevitable question of who chose to go there. But I had been invited into the fold of the family and had rubbed elbows with brothers proud of the roles they were to play in society. In Hugh's eyes, in some way, we had all failed her. I should have protected Catherine the way he had been sure I was able to, I should have made sure we would not be in a situation where what happened could occur in the first place. Things had turned out to be far different than either of us could have imagined.

Hugh finally dares to turn the conversation to me. "Here to get your passport?" he says.

I nod.

"You're leaving in . . . what is it, two months?"

"I hope to leave," I say. "But I may be required to stay."

Hugh nods as I think of all the conversations we have had, his gruff, ideological pronouncements about the gifts and trials of living. Now I can see that he has probably suffered quietly during the last few months and that the result of his suffering is uncertainty. I realize it now, that in this instance I am tougher than he is because I am used to thinking that bad things can happen to people like me. I think about all the struggles my mother has endured, as a child and as a parent and as a wife. She'd always thought that life was supposed to become easier and, instead, it became harder. My father's illness has kept my mother guessing for years when she would become a young widow, as she would be in a few more years, with very little money or help. Beyond this, during periods when my father had been incapacitated, my mother already experienced what life would be like as a single parent.

"WELL," HUGH SAYS finally, "the police shouldn't keep you here for that. The others can fill in."

"It's not so easy," I say. "After all, certain specific things happened to me that will have to be told to the court."

"Affidavits can serve that purpose. Sworn testimony."

And then I realize that besides being reassuring about my being able to leave New Orleans, Hugh might prefer that I miss the trial. My presence there might make it more difficult for him.

I go on, "Well, I guess I have to wait and see. The DA's office told me that they'd pay if the plane ticket has to be changed."

"But aren't you enrolled in one of those overseas programs?"

I nod.

"Then having to be in New Orleans, you'd be forfeiting too much. Maybe if we talk to Ms. Lombardino she can help us figure out how we can work around this."

I shrug and tell him that's not necessary, but he insists.

An uncomfortable silence falls and finally he asks, "Do you need a ride?"

"No," I came by bicycle. I point to my new Fuji.

He approaches the bicycle rack with me and looks at it appraisingly as he would look at a vintage car that catches his eye. "Nice piece of equipment. So these are your wheels in Rome?"

I explain that part of my fixed idea of life in Italy is being able to ride around the city. I had wanted to buy an Italian bicycle, of course, but in all the months working at the shoe store I had managed only to save enough money to buy a Japanese one. Hugh laughs. I can tell he is about to walk away. But then he suddenly grows agitated. "Look, Barry," he says. "I don't want to make a big deal out of this, but I just want you to know that nobody blames anybody in what happened at Audubon Park.

You've heard this, I'm sure, from Catherine. But I've wanted to tell you myself."

"Thank you," I say. I wait for more, expecting him to continue, to give me more to go on, but he doesn't. He shakes my hand, and as he walks away, a gust of wind comes in off the Mississippi and flaps the trousers and the jacket of his seersucker suit.

To PREPARE for my journey I begin cycling everywhere. I put my bike on the Canal Street Ferry, take the boat across the Mississippi from Old Algiers to the beginning of Canal Street downtown and go on long rides. I ride through the French Quarter, out Saint Claude Avenue to the Ninth Ward, where my mother grew up. I pass by the family's shotgun house on Dauphine Street in which both her parents died. The place has been repainted a bright pastel mauve by the Yuppie couple who moved into it. It was in this house, my grandparents' house, that I spent a lot of time as a small child—too much time, according to my mother, who claims that if her parents could have adopted me they would have. She used to fight with them sometimes because they'd want to have me stay on with them after having already spent the weekend without my brother and sister. I didn't help matters any by insisting on calling my grandmother every day when I got home from school. This devotion was mistaken for overriding affection. My grandmother would use this as a weapon against my mother and claim that I preferred living away from my immediate family. This was hardly the case, my calling my grandmother was merely a gesture on my part. I did it because I knew she liked it, not because I missed her.

I ride through the outskirts of the Garden District and the well-to-do university area, past De La Salle, the Christian Brothers Catholic boys' school that was firmly rooted in the old money society world in New Orleans and where I spent four years, occasionally dating debutantes and thinking I was from a more affluent background.

A week before I'm to leave New Orleans for my New York flight to Rome I am already anxiously getting everything ready for my trip. I tell myself that I'll take one last ride around the city and then pack up and won't ride again until I reach Italy. It is a very hot day in July, and I cut short my intended excursion to come home a bit earlier. I slowly pedal back to the ferry landing on the Mississippi and wait to make the ten minute journey across the river to Old Algiers.

The ferry arrives, unloads its passengers and soon we are summoned to board. I remember riding down over the steep ramp traversing the river and up onto the car deck of the boat, leaning the bike on the railing at the prow, so that I will catch most of whatever warm breeze there might be streaming off the river once the boat begins its crossing. Feeling hip and cool in my new sun glasses and the Italian cycling clothes that I bought with the few dollars left over from the purchase of my Fuji, I'm aware of several other people with bicycles. I favorably compare mine with theirs, feeling pleasantly tired, daydreaming, not really thinking or noticing anything else.

The ferry nears the dock, I mount my bike and move toward the exit ramp—bicycles are the first to disembark, before cars. I swing out and make a fast, gliding descent from the height of the levee, down to the street. I have the feeling of people riding behind me. I hear the metal ramp vibrating with the weight of other bicycles. And as I begin riding briskly along an old brick street that dates back to the nineteenth century, I have the sense of . . . it's almost like shadows, of more than one person riding close by and attempting to pass. And just as I begin to steer away from whomever it might be I hear something bang against me, but the sound is muffled and quickly fades. Then my vision suddenly narrows until anything I do see, any light, is merely a pinpoint. Then

I'm falling and my body slams against the hard surface of the street, the shooting pain of scraping asphalt, the taste of pebbles in my mouth, the sense of a liquid running down my face—but by now everything is dark. I feel hands trying to wrench the bicycle away. They yank at it and I hold on, and at one point manage to open my eyes and see a glob of blood and then hear my heart pumping in my ear. I close my eyes, thinking that if I keep them shut, my heart will slow and that all the blood won't pump out of my body. There's laughter and then screaming. And then the jolting explosion of a pistol.

Six

I HAVE NOW LIVED THROUGH two acts of violence. These events have become lodged in my psyche along with the constant lament that I could have done more to save Catherine from Zachariah Thomas.

I wonder, too, if I could have done more to save myself from the group of hoods who followed me off the ferry. Unlike the feverish recall of what happened at Audubon Park, the second violent incident unfolds more like a dream sequence of images that are reconstructed for me, when I regain consciousness in the hospital, by the doctor who put fourteen stitches in my head. He is the one who tells me that a housewife standing in her garden heard the commotion, came running out of her house, fired a gun into the air, and ended up bringing me to a hospital.

People who have never been victims of random violence assume that they can avoid danger and therefore be able to protect themselves in any situation. For many more, the thought of being at risk never occurs to them. They just make a subconscious assumption that they will always be safe. For Catherine and myself this sense has been obliterated. Beyond this, as time goes on, we both discover more and more cracks in our sense of well-being. That night at Audubon Park continues to haunt us, and will for a long time, and because of it, we both find ourselves separately spiraling downward into self-destructive behavior and lingering depression.

WHEN I FINALLY leave for Rome, I dream that a foreign country and a different life will put the horrors of what happened behind me. Catherine, unbeknownst to me, is entering into a relationship with someone I introduced her to, a guy named Jack. At first she believes that having a lover will help her withstand the continuing emotional fallout of the rape. But Catherine never quite realizes how difficult it would be for any young man, not even twenty years old, to deal with a woman suffering from nightmarish flashbacks of a sexual assault, often unable to cope with daily routines, someone who is dredging up a lot of terrifying emotions in her psychotherapy. Beyond this, the relationship highlights severe sexual conflicts, fears about spreading sexually transmitted diseases, and the inevitable associations with the memory of being raped.

FOUR MONTHS into my Roman sojourn, Sarah, a new friend of mine from the International University, convinces me to accompany her on a trip away from winter's dull gray drizzle. Together, we take the interminable train journey south to Sicily.

As we pass through the countryside just an hour away from Rome, the sun, which we have not seen in days, begins to fracture through the low clouds. By the time we are well south of Naples, the promises of Sicilian sunshine and warmth are more credible. We are imagining our exploration of Sicily's small towns, cities and back roads, which, to many travelers familiar with Italy is a somewhat frightening prospect. The island's mythical stories of bandits, its history as a Mafia stronghold, and warnings to women traveling alone keep many people from exploring its extraordinary natural beauty.

Any in-depth conversation I have with anyone invariably touches upon what happened in Audubon Park, and particularly now as Sarah and I address the warnings we have heard about traveling in Sicily. By now she has heard most of my story. But she hasn't heard what happened as I was riding off the ferry in New Orleans.

"You're really obsessed with Catherine and that crime, aren't you?" she comments impatiently.

"You would be too," I say, on the defensive. "If you had lived through it."

She looks away out the window and murmurs that this is debatable.

There is a curious competitive air between us and with that one remark her dismissal of this pivotal event spurs the same self-loathing I felt immediately after the crime.

SICILY SEEMS MUCH wilder, the countryside much quieter than the area around Rome. Carrying my new-found suspicions about strangers and unfamiliar places, I find the island immediately more menacing. It is perhaps the combination of the ragged, rocky coastlines with dramatic cliffs that plunge down to the sea and the tough, mountainous inland terrain coupled with what I fantasize are the unspoken conspiracies that may be taking place at any moment all around us in the still hours of the midday siesta when all of Sicily seems to be in repose. I can't help wondering if *la cosa nostra* is in control as much as it is rumored to be, or is it just a clichéd myth? Are those eyes peering out at us from behind closed shades, or is it my imagination?

As we exit the Taormina train station, a middle-aged woman wearing a matronly housedress with a black scarf over her head walks right up to us and says hello. Her expression is warm and open and sincere. Seeing we are tourists, and that we look lost, she invites us to her apartment a few streets away and offers lunch. After climbing several flights of stairs, we reach her door and walk into a huge apartment with many rooms and wide, startling views of the city and of distant mountains.

"You should take the bus there," she says after lunch, pointing a beautifully manicured finger out of the window, "and go up the mountain to get a better view of our volcano, Mount Etna." She motions toward the street where a rickety old blue Fiat bus is parked near the train station.

The bus is covered with dirt and dust, its windows slathered with a filmy substance. Bucking and vibrating its way up the steep and winding gravel road, the bus makes numerous local stops along the way to pick up mostly older women clad in black who are taking the long journey up the rugged road to market for the evening's dinner. It is the strangest landscape I have ever seen, almost lunar; and the land gets rockier, the population becomes sparser, the altitude more apparent as the air starts to cool slightly.

After nearly an hour, we arrive at our destination. This is the point from which we can hike up a steep dirt road and then maneuver a few confusing turns before we can find the good view of Mount Etna. We head up a walled and dusty stone road that is a much steeper grade than we imagined it would be; but after we have traveled it for about thirty minutes, it levels off and deposits us into another tiny piazza of an even smaller village.

Entering a narrow, dusty passage out of the main square, we run into a group of teenage boys, four or five of them, laughing and yelling and jabbing each other and adjusting their crotches. It is a particularly Italian, if not Sicilian, sight to see teenage boys traveling together en masse as they go through the rituals of macho posturing. And it is particularly Italian for teenage boys to gesture to their penises, gestures that can mean a variety of things from insults to the level of their sexual prowess.

WE CONTINUE up the path for another fifteen minutes, slowly realizing we are nowhere near our destination. As we begin to lose daylight, we also lose interest in gaining the outpost overlooking Mount Etna. We head back down. When we round a curve in the ancient stone road, we practically run right into the group of boys we had seen earlier. They are standing in a group, in tight formation, leaning against a stone wall, peering at Sarah with predatory eyes. All of them are smoking cigarettes.

When we walk past them, one mutters "putana," the Italian for "whore," in our direction. We keep walking, but the same voice, now joined by the others, yells the word again, and as we turn around to look at them, they have started to walk toward us, continuing to heckle us as they approach.

For a moment, I flash back to the Mississippi River when I could see from a distance the figure of Zachariah Thomas floating his way down the sidewalk along the river, when he was just a curiosity, before he became a threat. I can smell the treacherous river, I feel the muck on my feet as I hobbled out toward the dangerous water. I hear the buzzing sound of cicadas, the distant hum of souped-up car engines. But now I am not nearly as afraid as I was that night at Audubon Park. Now my fear easily feeds into rage.

My whole body is on alert as we continue walking to the mountain village where the bus originally dropped us off. We cross the sad, empty piazza. And then I see gang members walking on either side of us, hear ricochets of laughter and the ugly word twists out of someone's mouth: "putana."

ZACHARIAH laughing as he leaned over Catherine in the pickup truck, demanding that she tell him how many times she's had sex with a black man, making her describe fake encounters as he penetrates her with the barrel of his .38, asking again and again, "So what you gonna do with me, baby?"

BY NOW the gang has surrounded us in a bold, decisive move. And then it suddenly dawns on me that something is very similar. To Zachariah, as well as to them, I have become invisible. Fear of eclipse detonates rage just as I hear once again the word "putana."

Something clicks and I bolt at one of the boys, grab the back of his head with one hand and punch him square in the face with the other. Before the others try to come at me, I manage to still his flailing body, and pull him into a headlock. And then I fling him away from me with such force that he lands on his back. Miraculously, the group scatters.

IN AUDUBON PARK, I was paralyzed by fear, by the suddenness of an assault. I had never before been attacked. This time, in Sicily, the raw memory of my last encounter propelled me to strike first. The scars of the first assault helped me survive the second one. In a way, in Sicily, I had less of a chance of prevailing and yet I somehow did. It didn't matter that we were greatly outnumbered. It didn't matter that we easily could have been killed in the empty square.

Was it now a greater awareness of the possibility of death: that a bunch of kids were trying to take our fate in their hands? Then again, what other circumstance can compare to facing a loaded gun, feeling the cold, heavy metal of its barrel pressed into your cheek? What other situation could produce the same level of paralyzing terror? Is the specter of a violent death more mortifying than one from, say, finding oneself in a building on fire and not knowing if the smoke will kill before rescuers arrive? Or being a weak swimmer caught up in a rip tide, suddenly faced with the possibility of drowning.

In response to those dangers, one's fear is defined by a kind of chemistry. When you have faced the possibility of being killed accidentally, or murdered, you have a bodily response that is hard to convey to those who have never come face to face with such a perilous prospect. Those who have never been at the lethal end of a gun barrel and who bravely assert how they will foil anyone who ever accosts them have no idea of the power that fear can play in those moments. Fear is uncontrollable, huge amounts of adrenaline are pumping through the bloodstream causing thoughts to become murky and the heart to pound. Sometimes you can react and save yourself. Sometimes you are powerless.

Many years ago in New Orleans, a hair salon on the seventeenth story of a building caught fire. It was the middle of a busy workday, the flames spread rapidly and the combustion created a suction that sealed off the doors. Trapped inside, desperate to escape, nine women broke the outer windows and jumped to their deaths. One of them died pregnant. Only one person survived.

She had been an expert high diver in her youth, and dove, rather than jumped, out of the seventeenth floor window to an adjacent roof nine floors below where other women lay dead or dying. Somehow she did survive, although she broke nearly every bone and was in a full body cast for more than two years. When she was interviewed from her hospital bed and asked what gave her the courage to jump, knowing that she, like all the others, would probably die, she responded quite calmly, "Fear. I was more afraid of burning to death than I was of that roof waiting down there. I told myself down there was like the surface of the water, and that's why and how I dove. I looked down and saw the pregnant woman I had been speaking to a little while before had hit the roof and died almost immediately. I told myself she was waiting there for me. She had died and I would send myself to my own death, instead of waiting for fire to come and get me."

When I remember this story, I remember Zachariah appearing and brandishing the gun and realizing there was no time to figure out a way to escape as the threat of being shot became more and more real. What would I have done in the diver's situation? Would I have jumped, or would I have waited to be burned alive?

BACK IN ROME a few days later, a sense of calm that I have not felt in more than a year descends. For the first time in months, I feel like the chip on my shoulder that I have carried with me from New Orleans has either shrunken, or maybe fallen off completely. I feel no guilt, no remorse for my reaction to the group of boys.

An odd, unsettling euphoria had washed over me in that piazza, when the boys who were heckling us, and even when Sarah herself, looked on in disbelief. They all must have wondered where the rage was coming from; it was certainly not anything anyone could have predicted. Whatever it was, the shock of its swiftness was thrilling.

For I have finally lived a shortened version of the brutal fantasy I have been replaying in my head over and over. Somewhere along the twisting, rutted road I have found myself on since the night in the park, I have been searching for chances to get revenge and to rebuild a fuller sense of what was there before me in the world once, and what is there before me now that I am no longer an innocent.

Seven

EARLY OCTOBER 1982 and the case against Zachariah
Thomas is on the verge of going to trial. My parents call Rome
to say that the dynamic new assistant district attorney who has
been assigned to prosecute Thomas has decided that there is
enough incriminating evidence to obviate my returning to testify in America. With the long list of crimes committed against
Catherine, Paul, and Alex, the prosecutors feel they have enough
evidence to win more than one life term for Thomas, thereby in-
suring that he will spend the rest of his life in jail.

Linda Bizzarro, a new assistant DA, signed on to the case
when Maria Rossi resigned to take a job as a US Attorney in
Houston, Texas. Already known for her stirring courtroom arguments and for her ability to show a jury how it is possible to
think passionately and rationally at the same time, Linda Bizzarro has managed to gather statements from Alex, Catherine,
my brother and myself that are completely consistent: from
the identification of the photographs of Thomas, down to the

chronology of events that occurred that night in Audubon Park.

A trim, leggy Italian-American woman who grew up in New Jersey, Linda Bizzarro is a rapidly rising star in the DA's office. According to my brother, Paul, she can be tough and strident on one hand, and playful and flirtatious on the other. In our few phone conversations, Linda Bizzarro purrs how lucky I am to be spending my year abroad in Italy. Despite the fact that I am relieved to remain in Italy, I am surprised to hear that the DA's office has decided to drop the charges against Zachariah stemming from what he did to me. I understand their reasoning, as well as the fact that they would incur the expense of bringing me back from Italy. And yet dropping the charges against Thomas for what he did to me somehow threatens to trivialize what I have gone through. On one hand it fuels my anger; whatever retribution he pays will not take the crime against me into account; on the other hand I feel guilty about being unable to provide moral support for everyone else involved in the trial. For surely, they will endure the public humiliation of having to tell an open forum what happened in painstaking detail, details that will be embarrassing, most of all for Catherine.

Almost one year to the day after Zachariah attacked us, the trial opens with a large spectator audience and considerable daily press coverage. When Zachariah first committed his crimes, the New Orleans newspaper, *The Times-Picayune*, ran the story prominently in its metro section, using all of our names except Catherine's. Now that the trial itself is underway, daily details and nuances are reported on television and in the newspaper. Linda Bizzarro is quoted alongside the defense attorney, as well as some of the spectators.

My parents try to attend the trial every day. My mother is a courtroom drama buff obsessed with legal intricacies and nuances of court trials; she would have been happy serving her life out as a night court judge. Whenever she sits in on a trial, as she has often done in her life, she takes copious notes on the testimonies of each witness, and then later deconstructs them as she tries every night to put the pieces of the puzzle together from the day's session. If she had her wish, the judge would call her after every recess into the judicial chambers with the prosecutor and defense counsel where she would preside and advise all of them on what their strategies should be for the next day.

Because Paul, Alex and Catherine are Zachariah's victims, they are not allowed in the courtroom except for when they testify. As each of them takes the witness stand, they will tell virtually identical stories about the perpetrator's appearance, the things he said to them, the car he was driving, and the physical violations of their bodies. All through that night in October 1981, he committed one felony after the other: assault with a deadly weapon, attempted murder, aggravated rape, aggravated burglary, and battery. And because there were a few of us present that night, the felonious charges against him mounted quickly. Years later when I interview Linda Bizzarro, she will tell me that she knew then that there would be enough evidence against Thomas, even without a rape charge, to send him to prison for many years before he would have even a chance for parole.

On the day of Paul's testimony comes a particularly dramatic moment when Linda Bizzarro questions him about what he saw that night in the park. He tells the jury for the first time that he recalled seeing a package of Kool cigarettes on the dashboard of Zachariah's tan Chrysler Cordoba. The cigarette pack, I also noticed, has become a crucial piece of evidence. The Chrysler had been found parked on the street near Marla Bordeaux's house. The police officer investigating the scene had noted the Kool cigarettes on the dashboard in his report. When they finally arrested Zachariah, they had found his car keys, which fit the door lock and ignition of the Cordoba. Other personal items were also in the car, as well as one of Paul's credit cards.

When Paul told Linda that he recalled seeing the cigarettes, she introduced as part of the DA's exhibit a photograph of the interior of the car and its dashboard taken just after Thomas was arrested. A pack of Kools was visible in the photo. When the photo was presented to the court, an appreciative murmur rose in the spectator gallery, which prompted the judge to demand silence and order in the court. In addition to the cigarette pack, Paul's driver's license, which Zachariah had stolen along with other cards, had fallen onto the front seat of the car, and in a close-up photograph of the front seat Paul's license is plainly visible.

During his cross-examination of Paul, the defense attorney, a young African-American public defender named Alain Dupuy, becomes blatantly hostile. He infers that my brother is a spoiled, rich white kid privileged enough to attend an elite Northern college. Dupuy obviously doesn't know about our working class life or my brother getting scholarships to college.

"I understand, Mr. Raine, that the DA's office had to fly you down here to New Orleans all the way from New York City, is that right?"

"Yes, that is correct."

"And you are living in New York because you're going to college up there, isn't that right, Mr. Raine?"

"Yes, that's right."

"Is there any reason why you go to college up there and not down here where you grew up, Mr. Raine?"

Dupuy was reflecting a common sentiment in the South: a disdain of college students who flock north to be educated.

My brother now explains to the jury that he received a substantial scholarship to cover all four years and that my parents were not in the position to afford such tuition.

"Oh, I see," said the defense attorney. "Well then, Mr. Raine, if you qualified for a scholarship, then that must mean you're pretty smart, right? That must mean that you probably know all the answers to all the questions I'm gonna ask you."

Through the vapors of long-winded questioning, it soon becomes clear that the defense attorney is attempting to portray the charges against Zachariah as a racist attempt to crucify his client. He begins to lash out at my brother, attacking his impressive vocabulary, holding it up as irrefutable proof of Paul's white elitism.

Now an established criminal court judge, Alain Dupuy was, in 1982, a young public defender, a member of New Orleans' large, distinguished Creole community. For more than a century, Creoles have played a significant role in the culture and commerce of New Orleans. They are of mixed Spanish or French and African decent, usually with ancestral ties to the West Indies or other regions of the Caribbean. But in spite of their higher standing among blacks in New Orleans, the Creoles did not entirely escape the anti-black prejudice that has infected so much of the South during most of the twentieth century, even though the city of New Orleans was more racially harmonious in the turbulent 1950s and 60s than many other cities in the South.

It has often been said, and well demonstrated, that a significant number of the upper-class Creoles saw themselves as living in a higher order, apart not only from the old-money whites who reigned over old New Orleans society, but over the predominant, largely lower-class black population that could not claim Creole blood as the determining factor of their position in the culture. Mindful of their own long-established history in the city's upper echelons, many Creoles looked askance at the old-guard whites as well. The Creoles continued to ascend, their journey culminating with the election in 1978 of Mayor Ernest Morial, a Creole, the first non-white to hold the city's highest elective office. In short, Dupuy's firm grasp on his own superiority is evident.

At one point, he shows my brother an aerial photograph of the park. "I would imagine then, Mr. Raine, since you are a very intelligent man, you could tell me a thing or two about this photograph that would help the jury understand better where you kids were and where Mr. Thomas was the night of the crime." Paul dutifully points out the various locations, indicating the direction in which Zachariah fled after he forced us to wade into the river. "From what I can deduce," he tells the lawyer, "we were here and he was over here just a few minutes before he approached us."

The defense attorney raises his eyebrow in mock fascination as he looks at the jury. "Did you say you 'deduce,' Mr. Raine? You 'deduce,' is that right?" mocking Paul's use of what Dupuy thought was an antiquated, rarefied word. "I want to be sure the jury heard what you said. "Would you mind explaining for the jury here what the word 'deduce' means, Mr. Raine? Not everybody talks the kind of English you talk up there in New York." Amused by this, my brother asks the defense attorney, "Do you need the definition, or does the jury?" A low chuckle erupts from the area where the victims' families are sitting. It was at this moment, my mother recalled, during Alain Dupuy's questioning about the word "deduce," that Hugh, sitting in front of her, audibly murmurs, "Insulting." Hugh valued higher education, the power of language, and to have it belittled like this is no doubt a personal affront to him.

Later, Paul recalls his time on the witness stand. "As I sat there, Zachariah glared at me the entire time. He hardly ever took his eyes off of me." It is the first time Paul has seen the face of his attacker since the night when we'd caught a last glimpse of him through the windshield as he drove past in his flight from Audubon Park. At the trial Paul was surprised at how familiar

Zachariah looked, even though he had changed a lot since his arrest and certainly was trying to make himself look more clean-cut in court. "I kept trying to see the bloody splotches on his face, the ones in the mug shots at the police station that were taken after the police had beaten him up." In the courtroom Paul described Zachariah's "smoldering gaze" that looked as though he was ready to spring over the table and fly through the air to get him. "It was a little unnerving to be cross-examined by this defense attorney who had it in for me, to try to focus on what he was asking without making a mistake. And then keeping an eye on Zachariah as he was keeping an eye on me. I kept looking at the shackles around his ankles, wishing the chains were fastened around the legs of the table where he was sitting."

When Dupuy's questioning of Paul is finally over, the court goes into recess. My mother turns to discuss the harranging with my father, who waves her away and says, "I'm leaving. I have to get away from these people."

My father, now retired on disability from his various strokes, has been attending the trial with my mother. Every night when they arrive home, he calls one or two of his friends who used to work with him at the phone company and gives them an update. The night of my brother's testimony, my father parks himself in front of the TV, watching his normal spate of police shows and westerns, shows in which the bad guy always gets his due punishment. "Hawaii Five-O," "Mannix," "Dragnet," provide him with arrests and arraignments to revel in, long sentences served up to deserving criminals. Whenever my mother asks him a question, he shoos her away frantically, loathe to being disturbed. She knows that not only is he greatly troubled that the crime committed against his sons has become a public spectacle, he is particularly disturbed by the power Zachariah has over all of us. Later on, when I ask my mother to explain what she means, she says that the process of a trial gives the defendant a kind of dignity and attention. Look at how Alain Dupuy has treated Paul. A fair trial advances the notion that there is some possibility of acquittal. With all the questioning, with all the haranguing of the defense attorney against my brother, my father has become afraid that the legal system will turn against him. Against all of us.

Beyond this, my father has been put into the position of having to defend us, which means having to confront the whole question of masculine duty and how "all those guys" were overpowered by one man. Whenever the trial recesses, he disappears down the hallway, as though fleeing our shame. He has never interacted much with anyone, indeed he has had almost no friends. Whenever my mother mingles with other family members—her sister, my father's sister—discussing points of the trial, my father keeps to himself. If he strikes up a conversation, it is with one of the security guards that man the entrances. They are usually young black men. Despite what might seem like an outward prejudice my father speaks freely to the guards. He has always liked law-and-order men, and feels a kinship with them because of his years in the military.

Throughout the trial, various members of Catherine's large family come and go every day. Among seven brothers and sisters and their spouses, there is always a number of them present. Mr. and Mrs. St. Clair attend nearly every day and are certainly in attendance the next morning, the second round of testimony, when Alex the street hustler takes the witness stand.

He has found a suit to wear to his testimony, he has shaved and combed his hair. According to my mother, he cuts a handsome appearance, seems unnaturally poised, almost as though he is an Ivy Leaguer to-the-manor-born, scion of some privileged family rather than a trick-turning male prostitute. But then he opens his mouth to answer questions and his flat, hardscrabble New England accent betrays him. He's the one from the North, but his garbled, ungrammatical sentences, his prurient descriptions of what happened are the trashy low point of the trial.

Just as he had enraged the DA's office by disappearing in the days immediately following the crime, thereby slowing down the process of taking statements from all of us, Alex now infuriates Linda, the judge, and especially Hugh when he becomes flip and obscene on the stand. Sex is the only thing Alex knows, his only element of comfort and self-possession, and so he makes a point of describing in great graphic detail every single sexual nuance of the rape: the way Zachariah Thomas's ass looked as it was gyrating, the filthy humiliating words spoken to Catherine, the pumping violence of the one-sided act. And if this isn't enough, he actually chuckles and smiles as he doles out the dirty details. At one point, referring to when Zachariah ordered us to undress, Alex starts to laugh and says, "I stepped out of my fire-engine red bikini BVDs and I could feel a cool breeze rush up between my legs under my privates." All through his unsavory testimony, the defense attorney keeps making eye contact with the jury, a supercilious smirk scribed on his face, shaking his head as though to say that Alex's gleeful indiscriminate ramblings are compromising the prosecution's position. He falls as low as anyone can go and Dupuy has no need to try to take him down a few more pegs. It's only a matter of time before the witness will undermine his own credibility.

In the midst of it all, Catherine's parents shut their eyes and grip the bench as though they are on some harrowing amusement park ride. At one point Mrs. St. Clair becomes so upset that she jumps up from the bench and flees the courtroom gallery. According to my mother, Hugh at first gets up to follow her but then decides he must remain, and with a nod of his head, sends one of Catherine's older brothers. Finally he turns back to Alex with venomous attention, muttering curses under his breath, beating his fist against his hand. In the meantime, Alex taunts the courtroom with the idea that he has information they have all craved, that he holds them spellbound with his monologue. Finally, he is finished and when the judge asks the defense attorney if he has any questions to ask Alex, Dupuy, looking as though he is enduring a terrible odor, deliberately faces the jury as he says, "I don't think so, your honor. I don't think this witness has anything more to add than what he has already said."

On the third day of testimony, Linda Bizzarro calls Catherine to the witness stand. Wearing a conservative dress, little makeup, her hair pulled back from her face, Catherine looks pale and tense, and speaks in a low measured voice. According to my mother, in her relatively young career, Linda Bizzarro has achieved a perfect balance between knowing when she has to be hard-edged and when she has to tone down her questions to consider the delicate emotional condition of a witness. By the time Catherine timidly approaches the witness stand, she has developed a close kinship with Linda, a sense of mutual understanding and sympathy. But Linda knows too, that in the recesses of Catherine's mind, and in her emotions, there are deep scars and residual pain stemming from that night, and she is not entirely sure how far she can go in her questioning of Catherine without causing her to break down uncontrollably.

Linda begins by letting Catherine know that it is hard for her, too, to have to ask these questions, but that they are necessary to establish exactly what happened. The strategy Linda uses is wise because it establishes early on that she will build her case from a corroboration of stories of the other victims. But it also injects suspense into the proceedings because Catherine's testimony is really the one the jury and spectators are most waiting to hear. There is also the inherent drama of seeing a woman in person who has survived a brutal rape getting up in front of many people and telling them what happened to her. One looks at her, at her face and her body, one hears her voice, and inevitably tries to picture the degradation she went through. In some way, it is not unlike seeing a celebrity, who because of some horrible ordeal, becomes an object of gruesome curiosity. To finally hear the confirmation of the crimes from the person against whom they are committed, to hear them when she is sitting, face to face, just several feet away from the man who attacked her, is a final unsettling replay. Rapist and victim are there before the jury, together in public in the same room, and the images of that night in the spectators' and jurors' minds become more resonant. Every woman in the room knows that one day she could find herself in the same position in which Catherine found herself that night in Audubon Park.

"Ms. St. Clair," Linda intones, "the questions I am going to ask you here today are questions I would prefer not to ask. But they are necessary because they will help us establish for the jury what it was Zachariah Thomas did to you and the other three young men in Audubon Park on the night of October 10, 1981."

Catherine nods her head weakly in accordance.

"First, I want to clarify something for the jury. Mr. Dupuy has tried to put doubt in the jury's mind about why you were in the park with several young men, why you were the only woman there. Isn't it true that you have known these friends for some time and that you often spend time together with them?"

"Yes," Catherine says. "I have known Paul and Barry for several years, our families have been acquainted since childhood. However, Alex I met only recently. He is not a close friend of any of us, he is a new acquaintance who happened to be with us that night."

"So it is normal that you would be with these people in a group," Linda asks again.

"Of course," Catherine answers, "Paul and Barry are like brothers to me, that is how well I know them."

Linda goes on to establish various other details of that night, points that include how much time elapsed between when

Zachariah first spoke to us and when he finally walked away from us. She then begins to ask Catherine the specific details of what happened to her, what Zachariah said to her, what he was forcing her to do. In doing so she once again apologizes in a warm, sympathetic manner; however, the specific questions wear Catherine down very quickly.

Her poise and stoicism have stunned everyone who knows this case, everyone who has been involved from the prosecution side, as well as Catherine's friends and family, during the previous year. It is hard to remember that she is only 19; she has tried so hard to find insight and meaning, somehow, in this sad incident, to figure out what it means to her now and into the future. No one who has spent any time with her in the previous several months can recall her lashing out at anyone, saying anything racist or stereotyping a group of people, or showing any signs of being bitter or angry about what has happened. She is more bewildered than angry, wondering how she wound up in that position and why the randomness of life affected her as it did. Catherine is not shattered, but she looks wan, used up, and so it is all the more surprising that she is able to answer probing questions as strongly and as clearly as she does.

Linda continues. "Ms. St. Clair, can you tell the ladies and gentlemen of the jury what happened from the moment Mr. Thomas took hold of your arm in the several seconds that elapsed after he pointed the gun he was carrying at you and the guys?"

"Yes," Catherine says. "He told all of us to take off our clothes and to lie face down on the ground, in the grass. He told the guys to go to a certain spot several feet away from where he was standing with me. Then he made each of us empty our pockets, and we had to give him our wallets and whatever other valuables we had."

"And then?" Linda asked, conveying some silent signal so that Catherine knew what she wanted.

"He found a gun my father gave me."

Linda pauses, reflecting on this as though she has heard it for the first time. "Why did you have a gun?"

"My father insisted I carry it for protection."

"Is the gun registered in your name?" Linda asks.

"No," Catherine says. "My father's name."

There is a lull in the dialogue. "Please continue," Linda says.

"When the defendant found the gun he got angry at me. He took it away and then pointed it at me and at the guys. I was really afraid at that point that he was going to start shooting."

"And then?" Linda asks.

"Well, after he waved both guns at us, he took all our valuables and he ordered us to get undressed. He made the guys huddle close together, face down, in the wet grass, and he told them not to look up. The truck we were driving was parked a few feet away, facing us, and he dragged me by the arm over to the truck, got into the cab and pulled me inside with him. Alex thought that he was going to either drive away with me or attack me in the cab, and so he threw a gold chain that was around his neck. It landed in the back bed of the truck. Then he yelled that it was worth four hundred dollars. When the defendant heard the chain hit the back of the truck, he left the cab to find it. He was still holding on to me. He made me get out of the truck to go with him. In the meantime, Alex managed to jump up and run away and eventually brought back help. The defendant fired his gun at Alex, but he missed. The bullet just grazed his head."

"And what happened then, after Alex was able to get away?"

"The defendant got really angry. He ordered me to go into the back of the pickup truck and look for the chain. He stood there with the gun on me and watched the guys at the same time.

When I found the chain, I gave it to him. Then he made me get back into the cab of the pickup with him again."

Catherine stares at the floor, and there is a several-second pause where, knowing that a difficult stretch is about to start, Linda lets her compose herself for the roughest part.

"So, now you and Mr. Thomas are sitting in the cab of the pickup truck and Mr. Thomas still has the gun trained on you, is that right Ms. St. Clair?"

"Yes," she answers in a hushed tone, "that's right, and he starts talking to me and asking me a lot of personal questions about my sex life."

"What kind of personal questions?"

He asks me, "Hey, you ever had a black dude before?"

Catherine starts to cry. And then, as she tries to finish speaking, she trembles. "I said no. And then," she pauses for several seconds as she begins to cry harder, "he said well you gonna get one now." Catherine doubles over in the witness chair, her head buried in her hands, and all that is visible is the top of her head and her back heaving up and down with her sobs. She sounds as though she is gasping for air.

Linda has moved directly in front of the witness chair, in an effort to give Catherine a moment of privacy in this very public room. "Ms. St. Clair, do you need a few moments. Would you like to recess for a bit? Would you like to take a short break?"

Catherine miraculously composes herself enough to say, "No, thank you, I'm okay. "

Much later Linda Bizzarro will tell me that she had moved to the side and was about to continue questioning Catherine when she heard a hushed yowling coming from the court gallery. Mrs. St. Clair, sitting with several members of the family, is weeping openly, a linen handkerchief pressed to her face as she dabs her eyes every few minutes. Hugh stares ahead stoically, waiting for the testimony to move forward.

"Ms. St. Clair, you and Mr. Thomas are now still sitting in the cab. You have not left the cab again, and he is continuing to taunt you with personal questions. What is happening now?"

"He asks me if I like to 'give head' and he tells me I am going to do it to him. Then," she says in a tremulous voice, "he pulled down my underwear and penetrated me with the barrel of the gun, maybe three or four times, laughing and saying 'I bet you like that, baby,' and then pretending he's going to pull the trigger."

Once Catherine utters the word "trigger," a gasp erupts in the courtroom, and then after several seconds a low murmur which prompts the judge to call for order. The room quiets down. Catherine is still in the witness chair, crying, but she is sitting upright.

Linda approaches her slowly, looking as though she dreads the thought of asking any more questions. They look at each other and Catherine nods for her to proceed.

"So after Mr. Thomas penetrated you with the gun's barrel, what did he do?"

"He told me to open the right hand door and step out onto the ground. Then, pointing the gun at me and making sure I knew it was cocked and ready to go off the whole time, he jumped out behind me and with the gun shoved in my back, walked me back over to the grass where the guys were and told me to lie down on my back.

"Can you estimate how far away you were from the others?"

"Maybe ten to fifteen feet. Then after I lay down in the grass, he walked over to the guys and started kicking and beating them at random as he cocked and uncocked the gun and laughed."

"What were you wearing at this point?"

"A button-down shirt, underwear and socks."

"And then?"

"Then he walked back over to me, stood over me for a few seconds, unzipped and unbuckled his belt. He knelt down beside me, climbed on top of me. He pulled my underpants down to my ankles, and started having intercourse with me while he pressed the gun barrel into the side of my neck." Catherine's voice now is strong, steady, and she is not crying. Another murmur rises up from the audience before she continues. "He was very quiet then, really, but he was whispering and asking me if I liked what he was doing, and I lay there absolutely still. I did not try to resist, I was . . . limp like a doll. Even though he was on top of me, I was chilly. The river breeze was making me cold— that and the fact that the grass underneath me was wet. I was looking right into his face because I wanted to remember what he looked like. To remember that he had blemishes and pock marks. I remember thinking to myself that he looked really strung out and I wondered if he would've done this to me if he didn't take any drugs. He certainly smelled of alcohol and cigarettes, and had the body odor of someone who had not washed—in a few days, maybe."

By now, Catherine is working her way through her testimony calmly and with exacting precision. Her delivery is such that she leaves no doubt that what she is telling the court is exactly as it happened. Her recall and the return of her original poise are impressive.

My mother recalls the day of Catherine's testimony. "While she was testifying, I was thinking I have known this young woman for all these years, she was still a girl to me. But then I realized, now she isn't a girl anymore, not after having gone through this. She was an adult. She was playing a role in a place, in a scene I could never have imagined her inhabiting." When my mother told me, I in turn remembered the time Catherine was hired to work as a waiter at a high-end catered dinner for a local politician. On the day of the party, she had gone sailing, lost track of time and showed up an hour late to work. She arrived dressed in a woman's tuxedo, walked brightly into the dining room to report for duty and then realized she'd forgotten to bring shoes. She thought it was stuffy of the hostess to forbid her from working barefoot. I recalled that Catherine had also missed her high school graduation because she was late getting back from a jaunt to the Gulf Coast.

"Can you tell the court, Ms. St. Clair, what happened next. What did Mr. Thomas do once he was finished . . . raping you?" Linda asks.

"He stood up over me, and made sure I could see his genitals before he zipped his pants. By then, I think I was behaving like a zombie, and it was hard for me to give him any reaction to anything. I lay on the ground for several seconds as he stood over me. I think I was trying to carry myself to somewhere else, as far away as I could possibly be so I didn't have to deal with it. Then he threw my underpants to me, I put them on, and then he pulled me up by my arm and made me walk, still pointing the gun at my head, over to where the guys were. I kept thinking help was going to come any minute because Alex had been gone for what seemed like a long time. But it didn't. Then holding my arm, Zachariah started to kick the guys. They were still on the ground, naked and on their backs, and he kept pointing the gun at them and saying "BANG" and laughing each time he said it as he kicked them."

"Was the defendant hurting you then as well, assaulting you in any way?

"No, after he raped me, he was gentle with me. But he really wanted to show the guys that he had a lot of power over them. After he had done his damage there, after he kicked them in the legs and in the groin, he made us all get up and walk across the roadway to the grassy area along the river. Because of what he did to them, Paul and Barry had trouble walking. He made them lie face down in the grass again, and then he made me lie down and . . . he did the same thing to me he had done before."

Linda gently interrupts. "He raped you again?"

"Yes," Catherine testified. "He told me to lie down on the ground, on my back, and he took my underpants off and raped me again." A groan rises up from the court. Catherine begins to tear up again. But after a few minutes, she is sitting up straight and ready to continue.

"So, Ms. St. Clair, the defendant raped you twice in the course of several minutes, beat and kicked your friends, and still, after all of this time, he lets you know that he is not finished brutalizing and humiliating and degrading all of you. By now, Ms. St. Clair, how much time would you estimate has passed since Mr. Thomas first approached you and the guys and pulled out his gun?"

"I would think at least thirty minutes or more, although I am not sure."

"Would you say, Ms. St. Clair, that in addition to raping you and beating your friends and stealing your money and making you strip off your clothes and pushing you all down in the wet grass and threatening to kill all of you and firing his gun at Alex, that his plan was also to terrorize you, to traumatize you as much as he possibly could, to make you feel as worthless and as powerless?"

There was an objection at this point from Dupuy but the objection was overruled.

"Yes, I would certainly agree with that."

"He stayed as long as he felt he could to make sure he made you as miserable as possibe. Is that a fair assessment of what Mr. Thomas did that night, Ms. St. Clair?"

"Yes. In fact, when we all talked about it the next day, we couldn't understand why he didn't just leave after he had done what he wanted to do. Why had he kept laughing at us the whole time he was there?"

"What did Mr. Thomas do then, after he had raped you a second time, before he left the scene?"

"He stood over me and did what he did before with his penis. Then he zipped his pants again and pulled me to my feet, but this time he wouldn't let me put my underpants back on. I guess he wanted to humiliate me even more. Then, he made all of us walk down a short little path to the river where he pointed the gun at all of us and told us to walk into the water." Catherine trails off and begins to cry loudly, uncontrollably. According to my mother, it is, oddly, the most distressing moment of her testimony. For maybe a minute the courtroom is absolutely still and silent. While Catherine sobs, Linda looks tense, terribly on edge. Sure-footed as she is, Linda seems to want to show sympathy and respect for Catherine's emotional rawness, but is also acutely aware that the trial is at a critical moment and that, primarily because of Catherine's brilliant testimony, the prosecution will win the case against Thomas. She cannot let this moment slip by, nor can she badger Catherine with more questions as the witness dissolves in front of the whole room. Finally, Linda approaches the witness stand. They talk for several seconds. Catherine nods her head. Linda then speaks to the judge. The judge bangs his gavel and announces a fifteen-minute recess.

When the trial resumes, Linda opens by assuring Catherine that her questioning is almost over. "And can you tell me what happened after the defendant forced you and your friends into the water?"

"We waded until it was up to our waists. Then, Paul turned around and couldn't see Zachariah anymore. We all stopped, turned to look back at the shore, and he was gone. And I thought then, I am either going to drown in this river or I am going to walk back on shore and he will kill me there for disobeying orders if Paul is wrong and he's hiding somewhere watching us and we can't see him. But while I was walking back to the riverbank, everything that had just happened hit me. I was cold. I was wearing only a wet shirt. I was naked from the waist down, and I just collapsed in the water. Then I didn't care if I got sucked out and drowned. I had no more energy, I could not make myself take another step and I just wanted to sink into the current. I remember thinking that I had saved myself so far, how terrible it would be to drown out there. But then Barry and Paul came up and took each of my arms and brought me to the bank. I don't remember much after that, except the trip to the hospital in the police car for my examination."

"Thank you very much, Ms. St. Clair. That will be all, your honor," Linda tells the judge.

ALAIN DUPUY'S cross examination of Catherine is the classic one used in rape cases when the defense attorney tries to make the victim seem as though in some way she antagonized the rapist to the point where he was driven to attack her. Once Dupuy establishes her presence in the park that night, he asks her why she had been the only female in the group.

"Isn't it odd, Miss St. Clair, that you were the only female person among several young men on your outing in the park," Dupuy probes. "That there were no other young women with you?"

"No," Catherine says, "like I said before, it was not odd, because Paul and Barry are my friends, and because I often spend time with them. There were no other women there because our trip to the park was impromptu and whoever was together at the time, well, we all just went there together."

"But you would agree that it might look a little odd to the outsider to see all of these young men together with just you as the only woman," Dupuy presses.

"No," Catherine resists as her voice grow stronger, "don't ask me to say something I do not believe."

After asking her several other questions relating to the first time she spoke to Zachariah, questions about when the crime reportedly commenced, Dupuy says, "Now about this gun that you were carrying. The gun you *say* . . ." Dupuy stresses the word, "that Zachariah Thomas took away from you.

"Had you ever fired that gun?"

Catherine looks at him blankly. "At a person you mean?" she asks innocently, and there are titters in the courtroom.

"At a person. At an object. Please answer the question, Ms. St. Clair."

"My father taught me how to shoot the gun."

"And where was this . . . in your backyard?" Dupuy asks, glancing at the jury. There are more titters in the gallery.

"No, at a place where there are targets."

"Oh you mean your daddy took you for target practice."

"Yes."

"So you certainly knew how to use that gun."

"I knew how to use it, yes."

At this point, Linda Bizzarro objects to the defense attorney's line of questioning.

"Sustained," says the judge.

"My point, Ms. St. Clair, is that who's to say you didn't pull out your gun first, when you saw Mr. Thomas walking toward you. Who's to say that you didn't frighten him. That would make things a little different, wouldn't it?"

"Objection!" Linda Bizarro screams.

The judge is warning Dupuy about his line of questioning when Catherine speaks of her own volition, "It happened the way I said it did. Yes, I had the gun, and he found it when he went through our things. It made him angrier. But he was already angry."

"And why was he angry?" Dupuy says softly with a smirk on his face that suggests this, once again, is a question of race, and of have and have not.

"I honestly don't know," Catherine said.

Soon, Dupuy is pressing for details about the actual rape, asking Catherine to be even more specific than Linda Bizzarro had.

He tries to ask her about the various positions Zachariah put her in, about what he was saying to her, but these questions don't get very far because they are punctuated by Linda Bizzarro's barrage of objections.

Catherine had begun her testimony in a strong and determined voice, but as Dupuy digs deeper into the details of her memory, he chips away at her composure. Finally, after several minutes, when Dupuy, flippant as ever, asks another graphic question about what Catherine did sexually with the defendant, her voice cracks and she begins to weep. Dupuy is stomping on territory that Catherine has already tenderly revealed to the court during the prosecution's questioning. "Have some human decency!" Hugh cries out, at which point the judge gavels and calls a recess.

In a row opposite the St. Clairs, a sad-looking, meticulously dressed elderly black couple sits in the courtroom every day in the same place, wading through the trial, watching its proceedings with a stoical, forlorn air. For the first two days of the trial, my mother notices them but has no idea who they could be. They stand out not because they are black (many other black people attend the trial) but because of their faces, which she described as being "creased with worry, marked by years of working hard probably long past the time when they should have been able to stop." A long time later when my mother would describe the couple to me, she'd relate to them from the standpoint of her own life, once my father died (not too many years after the trial) having to work long hours, sometimes two jobs to keep afloat as well as pay off her own debts.

At the trial, my mother realizes the couple is probably either Zachariah's parents or close family members. But of course the lines between the two sides are drawn, and she feels it might be inappropriate to make a gesture when they would probably see their son or close relative sentenced to prison for the rest of his life.

Nevertheless, my mother points the couple out to Hugh, who hasn't as yet noticed them. He in turn begins observing them and quickly decides they must be the parents of Zachariah Thomas. During the impromptu recess during Catherine's cross-examination, Hugh approaches the Thomases who are standing at the end of a long, dark wood-paneled corridor just outside the courtroom. The white marble floors inlaid with honorary tributes to deceased lawmakers are a cool contrast to the warmth of the mahogany walls and the ever-present heat outside. Like any courthouse, the interiors of this one have the intimidating feel of officialdom, of high-ceilinged rooms sealed off by vaulting doorways and halls that dwarf the people who walk through them.

My mother watches Hugh speak to the couple. She cannot hear the conversation, but easily notices the "stricken" look on their faces when Hugh first addresses them. "Their expressions were anguished, fearful and embarrassed," she will tell me. Hugh's conversation lasts but a few minutes, but when he walks away from them, he looks somehow more at peace. The Thomases' faces, however, remain smitten with sadness. Many years later, Hugh will explain, "I told them that we all lost something that night in Audubon Park, but that their son had lost something, too. For all of us, it was the loss of innocence, the loss of the sense of safety and security. I told them I understood the pain that comes when a child goes wrong. And the anguish of having a child in prison for life? Unbearable."

When Dupuy's questioning of Catherine resumes, he is more respectful and tones down questions about the details of the rape itself. Watching it, my mother believes that during the recess his conscience rang a bell and he realized that he was committing untold injury to Catherine by trying to cast her testimony in a tawdry light. Soon, Dupuy tells the judge that he has no more questions.

Throughout the trial, Zachariah is never called to the witness stand to testify on his own behalf. Perhaps it is a foregone conclusion that he would incriminate himself, but for whatever reason, Dupuy never lets the jury hear from him.

Linda Bizzarro gives a spectacular closing argument, from which my mother quotes one memorable point: "Ladies and gentlemen of the jury, you may hesitate to convict this man of his crimes and send him to life in prison because, like all good people, you hesitate to take away another person's freedom. But don't forget, that night in Audubon Park, Zachariah Thomas sentenced a young woman to the prison of her memory and she will have to live with that memory for the rest of her life."

In his summation, Mr. Dupuy wastes no time trying to portray us, once again, as privileged rich white kids who came into the world with all the advantages the Thomas family has always lived without. It's hard for my parents to believe he dares to use this argument because it is so obviously untrue. Alex's background speaks for itself, but my brother and I are both working for our college education, for what is not provided by scholarships and loans. Yes, Catherine's family is comfortable and gentile, but in their rambling ranch house, they are not nearly as wealthy as the oil-rich and cotton-rich and rice-rich families who have Garden District mansions and plantations where they spend weekends, Colorado ski houses and New York City apartments.

Mr. Dupuy also keeps referring to Catherine as the only "token female," implying that we all had too much to drink and that we had taunted Zachariah Thomas, who had certainly not premeditated an attack. Next he brings up Catherine's "curious possession" of a handgun, which he feels speaks for itself. Then Dupuy makes the preposterous supposition that we tried to pin a crime on Zachariah that someone else had committed because we wanted a scapegoat and he was, by coincidence, the most convenient one. Indeed, this last point is insulting; however, it is obvious to everyone that Dupuy's arguments are weak, and that few people in the courtroom agree with what he is saying.

At the end of the long trial week during which I have been getting daily reports in the form of telephone calls from Paul, the hallway phone in my dorm rings at two o'clock in the morning. One of my dorm mates answers it and comes to wake me up. Paul is calling to tell me that Zachariah has been ultimately convicted and given a life sentence for rape, as well as four concurrent 99-year sentences for armed robbery, in addition to several other charges. He will never be eligible for parole.

I remember standing there, looking out my window, past the corner of the ancient several-century old ochre-colored building in which I live, past a tall cypress tree casting long moon-lighted shadows. In the distance, I can see the rolling body of the Tiber River and a few of the ancient Roman churches. All along I have expected a conviction and feel relieved, but not nearly as relieved as I think I should feel.

But then in my groggy state, I remember something. "Wait a second," I say to Paul. "Whatever happened to Marla Boudreaux?"

There is a trans-Atlantic silence on the other end of the line and then my brother cackles. "I can't believe I forgot to tell you."

"You haven't mentioned her at all."

Paul apologizes and then explains.

From the very first day of the trial Marla Boudreaux makes herself present at the court, fully expecting to testify. She keeps pacing restlessly up and down the corridor outside the courtroom murmuring her rendition of the story she has already told the DA and the police department a year earlier. She has taken this opportunity to dress herself as fashionably as she knows how, wearing a formal, frilly lavender dress cut low off her shoulders which matches the lavender ribbon wound through her white blonde hair and tied in a large bow just above her forehead. She also wears severe white spiked-heel boots that stop just below her knees. According to Paul, the effect is a study in *tart wear*, hardly anything resembling fashion. And as Marla clicks her heels up and down the corridor, reciting her monologue, she chain-smokes her way toward her big moment on the witness stand. "You could tell Marla was proud of how she looked," my brother chortles.

Marla has already been told that she might not be called as an official witness in our case because Zachariah's assault on her is legally classified as a separate crime entirely. But she apparently has heard this admonition as encouragement to show up at the courthouse, to be ready to testify in case the wind of potential questioning should change. "I'll put that som'bitch under the fuckin' jail," she tells my mother and a group of Catherine's family during a recess. Such language always makes Catherine's mother turn red with embarrassment, and she immediately retreats from Marla to a nearby chair, shaking her head as she nervously plants a cigarette in her tortoise-shell cigarette holder. (Marla was the kind of woman who Mrs. St Clair would have pronounced "common as pig trash.") Marla goes on, "And if they lemme near 'im, I'll whup his ass so bad, I'll kill 'im right in this courtroom here," between drags on her many cigarettes that are planted between her two fingers, not inside a cigarette holder.

"What kinda shit is that?" she asks when, after two days of pacing the hall she is finally told by the prosecutors that she will not be able to testify in our trial. "What the hell are these courts for? You know and I know the same guy done to me what he done to these kids. All I wanna do is tell the story like it is. The more people ya'll got," she tells Linda Bizzarro in the hallway, "the more that fucker's gonna fry." Marla is rooting for the death penalty.

Linda Bizzarro, ever unflappable, asks Marla to sit down on a bench, and they talk seriously for several minutes outside the courtroom. Years later Linda will explain that she wanted to be patient with Marla whom she would need for future testimony if they were to try Zachariah for other crimes. She wants to show

Marla that she respects her conviction. Besides such practical considerations, Linda, like all of us (as well as all the police officers involved), has grown to like Marla, who is personable, street smart and soulfully honest. She has clearly lived a hard life without relying on anyone else to pay her bills. She's always struck me to be a woman without fear, self-pity, guile, or suspicion, someone who takes on all aspects of her turbulent life as they come at her.

"We all wanted to take her into our lives, to make her life easier," Catherine would recount to me much later. After all, Marla Boudreaux was also the person who, with a frozen beer can, had stopped Zachariah from carrying on his rampage. "But she knew how to live no other way. She just kept moving forward," Catherine would say.

After the disappointment of being barred from testifying, Marla Boudreaux continues to show up at the court house every day for the rest of the trial, determined to be there when the verdict is announced. "I tole ma boss I had to work nights all this week so I could be here," she says to Paul. "I tole him there was no questions asked. And he didn't gimme no lip, no sir. He knew better than that."

When the verdict is finally read and word leaks out in the hallway that Zachariah will be in jail for the rest of his life, Paul happens to be standing with Marla who cheers, "Ya damn straight ya goin' to jail, honey. You sure as hell ain't comin' over to ma house again, I can tell ya that. No more cole burrs fer you, mister. Adios, amigo, and say hi to the boys for me." Cackling, she turns and kisses my brother on the cheek. "Gotta go to work. Ya'll call me if ya'll need anything. Ya know where to find me." Then she walks out of the courthouse, fluffing her hair as she passes the security scanner at the doorway. "Don't got no weapons on me, honey, not today," she says to the security guard as he spot-checks her. "Jus' my bare hands," she laughs, as she pushes open the big double doors and struts out into the sunlight.

Eight

THREE YEARS LATER in 1985, I'm staring out of an airplane window, down at a flat, unchanging landscape of interlocking swamps and estuaries. To one side is the seemingly endless plain of Lake Pontchartrain. On the other side, heading west beyond the approaching airport, is the wide, formidable Mississippi River snaking its way around New Orleans, its legendary eddies and tricky cross currents shimmering in the midday sun and heat. After having finally moved away from New Orleans, I am now returning from New York, one year later, to attend my father's funeral.

Before the mini-strokes and long hospital stays had begun to debilitate him, before he declined into a cantankerous invalid in his last year, my father used to launch into rhapsodies about the extraordinary engineering feats that were needed to protect flood-prone New Orleans from being engulfed by the prodigious amounts of water from all the marshes, wetlands and major bodies of water that hug the city. He used to tell me about all the bizarre, indigenous life forms that lived in the swamplands and which, like yeast, became more active during the city's long spells of searing heat during the summer and, intermittently, throughout the rest of the year. Lying several feet below sea level, situated in a sort of ever-expanding, elasticized bowl, New Orleans' contours change with the frequent stirrings of the marsh gases below the earth's surface. Built on a depression, hurricane-prone New Orleans is one of the worst places to ride out the winds and potentially catastrophic floods that accompany all tropical storms.

At 7:00 that morning, my brother Paul had woken me up with the news of my father's death, which did not come as a complete shock. A year earlier, my father had had a crippling stroke that left him paralyzed below the neck. Unable to speak, to sit or to feed himself, he'd been lingering in a nursing home. Unfortunately, throughout the past year his mind had remained lucid enough that he was able to understand everything that was happening to him: his body gradually shutting down and ceasing to function until he died of what was called general failure. His death was particularly sad because he had spent so much of his life in self-created misery and negativity; his last year ended up mirroring what he had prophesied for himself during his whole life. But perhaps he was lucky because his overriding pessimism allowed him to die unaware of all the wonders of life he had missed along the way.

DRIVING FROM the airport, I realize that any prolonged absence from New Orleans makes it feel foreign. Despite the fact that I'd grown up there, I'd always felt, even as a young kid, that I was a stranger, lurking at the fringe, gazing yonder, dreaming of other places. I did not harbor an intense dislike of New Orleans, I just felt that I belonged somewhere else, and no matter what I did to try to change this feeling, it had never left me.

I cross a bridge that spans the Mississippi to what the locals call the West Bank. Up until the early 1980s, when another bridge was built to realize the city's plans of having one bridge each for traffic flowing to and from the city, there was only one four-lane bridge which was routinely engorged with legendary traffic jams. "The Bridge," as the single, four-lane span was known, a term uttered by many citizens with dread and loathing and, sometimes, fear, is in many ways a symbol of the locally minded nature of New Orleanians. Scores of the city's suburbanites who live on the West Bank readily admit, and often with great pride, that they have not crossed "the bridge" in years. It is their only route out to culture and the larger world of downtown New Orleans, small as it is, yet many are happy and satisfied that all their needs are met in the sprawling, soulless, culture-free "Anywhere, U.S.A." strip-mall world that characterizes these suburbs as it does numerous other such locations outside of major cities around the United States.

However, New Orleans is one of the world's more self-satisfied cities. Owing to its reputation for good food, music and its insular, indigenous culture, as well as its family-oriented social structures, the city's residents often frown on natives who choose to live elsewhere after they have grown up there. What else could one possibly want from life that does not already offer itself, open-armed, as it does in New Orleans? It is a similar, pervasive purview that many natives have always used to see distances within the metropolitan area, driveable in twenty to thirty minutes from, say, the West Bank to Metairie, another suburb across "the bridge," as interminable, epic journeys. Indeed, in my own family, one of the reasons for the numerous estrangements from some of my aunts and uncles is the fact that we lived "so far away," which in New Orleans parlance meant a twenty minute, effortless, straight shot, high-speed drive on major interstates. To many residents, at least in my extended family, the prospect of such an odyssey defeated them at the start. And so "the bridge" plays a major role in the city's life by keeping its insularity intact.

But like San Francisco's Golden Gate Bridge, "the bridge" is also a favorite spot for suicide jumps into the Mississippi's murky brown vortex that lies hundreds of feet beneath the span's roadway. While I was growing up, I knew four people who clambered between the girders and leapt to their deaths. The most memorable was a neighborhood doctor's wife, a glamorous blonde who on a mild February morning went shopping at the Winn-Dixie supermarket in a full-length mink coat. Later that day, Mrs. Taylor drove to the top of the bridge, stepped out of her idling black Cadillac sedan and, clad in a wool suit and her mink, climbed over the railing and fluttered down into the river.

On the West Bank, where suburban housing developments and malls have been sprouting from filled-in marsh land since the 1950s, oak-lined suburban streets punish the sturdiest of cars and curbside signs warn motorists to travel at their own risk over the shards of cracked concrete slabs, that, propelled by the miasma of subterranean gases and oversized tree roots bursting forth from the landfill, are forever rising up from the ground. Traveling these undulating streets across such flat terrain, it is easy to see why present-day civil engineers say no city should have ever been erected on such unsettled land.

My mother breaks down when she sees me but then quickly composes herself as she, my brother, my sister and I begin to speak of funeral arrangements. Adhering to tradition, neighbors keep arriving with covered dishes of food so that we won't have to think about cooking. Bottles of soda pop and fruit juice are left on the porch along with pots of gumbo, jambalaya and cornish game hens. The phone keeps ringing with condolences from my father's relatives, some of whom we haven't heard from in more than twenty years. At some point, in our preparations for the funeral, my brother, my mother and I can't help but be amused by all the people we haven't heard from in years swarming to attend a funeral. We remark that Cajuns in particular, and those of French Catholic south Louisiana stock in general, love a good funeral and will travel hours to be present at the graveside of somebody with whom they've been out of touch for decades.

As we plan for the funeral services, my siblings, my mother and I smack up against the bulkhead of what will be expected by our family and friends: a religious service. My mother, who was raised Catholic and who with my father went through a brief period of fundamentalism, is no longer a churchgoer in the strict sense of the word. This is a remarkable transition on her part, one that my brother, sister and I have followed with a mixture of respect and awe. We all know how pervasive and fervently public religious faith is in the South. In the North, I have learned, religion is a more private, individual aspect of life. In the North, no automatic assumptions are made that all people must have some foundation in a religious tradition, or that you have to be Christian to be considered a moral, upstanding member of society. In the South, the words God and Jesus and Heaven are forever being thrown at you. In the South, one's religion seems to be one of the first snippets of information to be exchanged upon meeting someone new, as though establishing eligibility for exclusive membership in The Righteous Club.

Although my mother is single-minded in her own beliefs, she decides to defer to the majority of the mourners and asks a Catholic priest, an old friend of my father's, to eulogize. During the funeral service, which is packed to capacity, I listen to Father McCool tell stories about my father, adding testimonies to his character. Whatever sadness I feel is blunted by the great distance that grew between my father and myself as I made life choices (which included living in the North) that he neither understood nor supported. I feel as though I'm hearing a sermon about somebody I barely knew. My eyes have been dry since I've arrived.

When we finally file out to a waiting limousine along with several other family members for the short trip to the cemetery, somebody grabs my forearm. "Hey," Catherine says in a low, subdued voice.

She's standing at the curbside with Mrs. St. Clair. They are both wearing black dresses, the fashion simple but undeniably appropriate and understated. I notice the way they are both poised, sympathetic, ready to lend their support. Mrs. St. Clair crosses to take my mother's hand and gives it a squeeze, whispering a few words of comfort. Once Catherine and I embrace, she confides to me, "You know, I always liked your dad.

"I know he was gruff and difficult," she says. "But I also think he was often misunderstood.

"For one thing he had a sense of humor. He let it out with me a few times. He used to make me laugh."

For example, Catherine goes on to say, during the trial my father imitated the defense attorney in such a precise yet exaggerated way, that everybody, Hugh included, would howl with laugher. I notice that she speaks of the trial as though it just ended recently.

Yes, of course. I remember my father, when he fell off that telephone pole and spent so much time in the hospital, used to play the clown to amuse the other hospital patients, blessing them with good humor.

I watch the weather on Catherine's face changing as something urgent arises, something that I instinctively know has nothing to do with my father's death. "You have time before you go back?" she asks.

"I could make some."

"Need to talk to you," she says nervously, barely able to get the words out. "Can you meet me at Figaro's?"

In below-sea level New Orleans, bodies are interred in above-ground vaults. This practice was begun many years ago when, during heavy rains, buried caskets would rise to the surface like buried automobile tires. Citing health hazards, laws were passed that prohibited the deposition of any bodies directly into the ground. And so was born the New Orleans architecture of mausoleums, of alabaster mini-mansions adorned with statuary and putti, the designs and splendor of the crypts appreciating until New Orleans cemeteries eventually became some of the city's most popular tourist attractions. Wealthy families competed against one another in terms of whose burial monument was most imposing. For the less affluent, large vaults stacked five or six levels into the air accommodate multiple decedents. As I watch my father's simple gray coffin being hoisted by hydraulic lift to its final resting place high in a wall, I remember how once, a long time ago, his own mother continually beleaguered him to make sure she was buried low down in the pile so that her body would be shaded from the frying sun.

THE NEXT DAY at Café Figaro, an outdoor café in New Orleans' "uptown" district, I notice that Catherine's famously lovely skin is full of blemishes, something I hadn't registered at the funeral.

"Pretty, isn't it?" She picks up on my concern. "It's nervous skin. Every time I break up with somebody, my face shows it." We're drinking wine and she's compulsively fingering the rim of her wine glass. I wait for her to elaborate. She doesn't and finally I ask her if she's had a lot of boyfriends.

She nods and explains that she is suffering from a serious— side effect, she calls it—from the rape. Once intimacy leads to sex, she finds herself seizing up and "freezing out" the man with whom she is involved. Then she smiles at me grimly. "But that's not a surprise, is it, Barry, because this thing still haunts me. I think it's going to haunt me forever. How many years since the trial?" she asks me.

"Three," I say without hesitation.

"Seems like my whole life, those three years," she murmurs and takes a large sip of white wine. "My therapist says I'm expecting too much of myself."

"Maybe you are."

"And what about you?" she said. "Does it still affect you?"

I tell her that sometimes in New York City, late at night when I'm walking alone in the streets, I find myself growing extremely anxious, always on alert, waiting, expecting something to happen. I tell her that I take extra precautions; for example when I'm waiting on a subway platform I always make sure to stand near a group of people. And even once I am riding the subway, I will leave a car that is populated by less than three or four passengers. It's the sense of being in a deserted, public place that makes me the most anxious, because I was in a place like that when Zachariah Thomas appeared with a gun strapped to his leg and a menacing glaze in his eyes. I tell her that none of my Manhattan friends believe that New York City is a much safer place to live than New Orleans.

"Well, I have frequent flashbacks," Catherine confides. "I think I have gotten about five good nights of sleep in the past few years. And I do have moments like you when things get too quiet and I find myself feeling panicked."

She mentions Jim, a mutual friend, a totally benign sort of guy who rides his motorcycle anywhere he goes and when he rides always dresses in a black leather jacket and jeans. One night Catherine was expecting him for dinner. At the designated time, her doorbell rang. She went out in the hallway to make sure it was Jim, and when she saw the black jacket and black jeans she screamed, ran back into her apartment and, despite his entreaties, locked him out.

Catherine takes a large slug of wine and then admits to me, "Other things happened. I haven't told anybody about."

"What do you mean, things?"

Her face caves in and tears start in her eyes. "The things he did to me."

Hearing the explanation that follows her cryptic remark, I'm suddenly thrown back into that febrile paralysis beyond fear, the state when, vanquished by a gun, I am lying in the dirt smelling the river mud. The things he did to her were different than the things he did to me. When he put a gun to my back and made me wade out into the Mississippi until the brackish water came up to my neck, when I could feel the treacherous currents tugging at my legs.

"Like he kept forcing me to say over and over how much I wanted him. Like when he was starting . . . to rape me, he ground my face into the grass, to make it hurt to make it as uncomfortable as possible so that in the midst of it all, he could degrade me."

Yes, of course. It wasn't enough that he brutalized us, he had to make us feel ashamed of our weakness, of the fact that like moths he caught us and now would watch the heat singeing our wings before he threw us to the flames.

"Jesus Christ, Barry!" Catherine says in a voice that's so loud it hushes the people lunching around us. "He was so strong, my God. I couldn't even do anything. It was like being squeezed in a vise. I've never felt such power in all my life. And it was evil."

I reach out and take her hand. "I know exactly what you're saying."

"And the thing that's been driving me crazy," she continues, "is I keep thinking that maybe the women who get raped get raped because they give off something. Maybe it's a certain kind of look, not necessarily sexual, but some . . . attribute that triggers something in men who are depraved. And it's only a matter of time before these women like myself end up being the target of men like him."

The waitress comes and sets down her plate of fried calamari. Catherine ignores the sizzling, breaded rings and sits there breathing hard. Finally she says, "This is not a healthy way to think. In fact, I think it's pretty twisted."

I'm feeling sick in the pit of my stomach. And this nausea soon curdles into rage. Rage at what this man has done to both of us. Suddenly, it's no longer enough that Zachariah is in prison. Once again, my fantasies run to revenge, about him being tied down by his fellow inmates and being forced to submit to a sodomous act of an excruciating intensity, and that in his state of agony he will be forced to think back on all the harm he gleefully inflicted on us.

Nine

VIOLENT CRIME HAS FOR YEARS been as much a part of New Orleans as its reputation for being Fun City. Anyone who lives in New Orleans and participates in the many indulgences it offers learns the city and knows how to maneuver through the checkerboard map of "good" neighborhoods and "bad" ones. Keeping out of troubled areas requires some nimble-footed dancing, and savvy residents know how important it is to master those steps. The city is frequently on the top of the list of America's most crime-ridden cities. It has spent many years as the #1 city on that list, and that dubious placement has long been associated with the notoriously corrupt New Orleans police department, for many years one of the lowest paid law enforcement organizations in the country.

Summer 1995 brings a long-simmering national obsession with rampant police corruption all over the United Sates, but many of the most lurid stories trickle out of New Orleans. Having begun to make my way as a fledgling journalist over the last several years, I manage to flag the interest of a British newspaper editor who assigns me to write about New Orleans' morally contaminated city government and its law enforcement establishment in the wake of a recent police corruption scandal rocking the city. Up until the Antoinette Frank case, the main story of corruption was police officers double-crossing each other for the money they were making with drug dealers for whom they worked as security guards to protect warehouses full of supply.

Antoinette Frank, a young patrolwoman and her young male partner, a married father of three, shared a moonlighting job providing security for a Vietnamese restaurant in New Orleans East, home to many Vietnamese immigrants. One night, the patrolwoman, off duty from both her jobs, staged a robbery of the restaurant with an accomplice. Not only did she murder two hard-working siblings of the Vietnamese family, she also accosted her police officer partner who was on duty as the security guard and shot him to death. In a perverse twist, Antoinette Frank reported the crime, went home, and then returned, as though she were an off-duty officer responding to a call for assistance. However, unbeknownst to her, a son of the restaurant owners had eluded her and her accomplice and hid in a walk-in freezer whose windowed door offered a clear view into the restaurant's dining room. Shivering and petrified, he witnessed the entire scene. Once he gave his account to the police, Antoinette Frank vehemently denied having any participation in the crime. But finally the pressure grew too much for Frank and she was forced to recant. Charged with the murder, she eventually went to trial and was sentenced to death.

The assignment requires me to spend time in New Orleans, conducting interviews, reading court records about the Antoinette Frank case as well as other police corruption cases in the archives of the New Orleans police department and the criminal courts building. After spending a few days deep in the bowels of a filing room, I am once again surrounded by thoughts of trials, testimonies and criminals.

The file storage system in the New Orleans criminal courts building is astonishingly archaic, its scattershot order overshadowed by utter chaos and inefficiency. My research quickly deadends and I can't help wondering if the widespread corruption that I seek to uncover is further corrupted by what seems like a bankrupt filing system. Frustrated and fired-up, I ask one of the filing clerks about the rape case records in which I appear, documents that are now more than ten years old. I learn that because of their age, they are stored in another building that requires a special request form. On a whim I fill it out and continue my research into police corruption. Finally, I gain access.

Reading through the records of the rape case at long last, I fully expect the details will turbocharge my memory, but what happens is a shock. The police report actually contradicts many of my strongest recollections.

For one thing I read that after a night of carousing we'd actually arrived at Audubon Park at midnight and the crime itself happened shortly thereafter. How can this possibly be true? Even now in my mind's eye the events break at twilight, eerie light infiltrating the brambles of the Butterfly, as the butt of the gun is shoved in my back, as Zachariah takes a whimpering Catherine into our pickup truck, as Alex rips the gold chain from his neck and tosses it through the air. I can still remember wading into the wide river, looking at its surface darkening but still cradling the last of the daylight. I remember hugging Catherine in the parking lot, and spying a car in the distance, a tan Chrysler Cordoba driven through the dusk by Zachariah himself who slows down in his approach and passes us grinning wildly. Rather than doubting myself, I have to wonder if somebody actually rewrote the file to make it seem more dramatic, more lurid. It says, "Suspect drove past the victims at 2:10 a.m."

Again, how can this be possible?

I uncover more and more facts about the case that I had not known before, about the other crimes Zachariah committed during his drug-induced violent spree that night in 1981. I realize that the police made it their business to keep us ignorant of the other acts of violence so as not to influence our testimony. But it soon becomes clear that his agenda that night was to attack and rape and humiliate as many people as possible before ending his rampage.

Once he left us and before he arrived at Marla Boudreaux's house, he accosted, at gunpoint, a group of four college students who were leaving a bar. One of the students, a young woman, was walking ahead of her three friends to unlock her car when Zachariah appeared from the shadows, grabbed her in a headlock and dragged her screaming down the street. By the time her friends realized what was happening, he had already locked himself and the woman in his car, waving his gun at the abducted woman's head as a warning for them to stay away. Luckily, just at that moment a police car responding to another call came barreling down the street, making Zachariah assume that they were in close pursuit. He pushed the woman out of the car and drove off but, for some inexplicable reason, returned to the same block of the same street where he had assaulted the young co-ed. There lived Marla Boudreaux, who after he forced his way into her house offered him a cold beer and cold-cocked him with it.

"I BELIEVE he is at Angola," says Linda Bizzarro, our heroine district attorney. She refers to Louisiana's notorious maximum-security prison north of New Orleans. "That's where all the worst guys go." She laughs. "You can call there if you're trying to track him down, but you probably won't get very far with them. There are too many lines of protection set up against the press. What is it that you want, anyway? Why do you want to interview him?"

"I'm not sure," I tell her. Although it is something that I have begun to consider, sitting face to face with the man who, in a certain way, has had the most impact of anyone on my life. That he is who he is is in itself a story, a story of a crime victim confronting the person who perpetrated the crime against him. The story of what somebody like me might bring to such a meeting and all the emotions that it involves. Taking notes on myself and my reactions might be just as important as taking notes on his. But it seems to me that, besides Catherine, he is a huge part of this.

"Well, you don't really think that you're going to get a confession out of him fourteen years after the fact," Linda says. "More than likely he'll probably claim he doesn't remember you and that he was unjustly put in prison."

"Well that doesn't make a difference to me," I say. "Because I know the truth. I remember what he looks like."

WHEN I CALL Angola and speak to the clerk who controls the flow of information to the press about prisoners, she tells me there are no less than four prisoners at Angola who have the name Zachariah Thomas. None of the birth dates she has for these prisoners correspond to the birth date I retrieved from his police records. After several phone calls back and forth to Angola, and several more to request his police records to double-check the birth date, I learn the dates recorded originally in the police file were incorrect because Zachariah had lied to the police before they were able to locate his driver's license. I give the clerk the information about the crime he committed, the docket number and the date of the crime to check it against the records kept by the prison. Finally, they are able to match me with the correct Zachariah Thomas.

"This Mr. Thomas," says the clerk at Angola, elongating the name in her north Louisiana drawl, "is in solitary confinement." Apparently he'd been in there several weeks now for brutalizing another inmate. According to the clerk, he has a long record of such bad behavior at Angola, and it's not his first time in solitary.

"And do you have any idea when he'll be out of solitary?"

"Probably another few weeks or so. But why do you need to know this?"

"I was thinking of visiting him."

"For what reason?"

"To interview him. I'm a journalist."

"Well, we just don't let anybody go and visit the prisoners. For one thing the prisoners have to agree. And I'll tell you what, he's going to want to know why."

"I'm trying to write a book that touches on his life."

"Well before you get in to see him, if you get to see him at all, you're gonna have to be a lot more specific than that."

And then, fearing rejection, I tell her that my thoughts are not quite formed and she suggests I get back to her when they are.

A few days after my conversation with Angola, I am combing through the criminal courts records when I strike what is the equivalent of archival gold: a cache of legal papers, briefs and petitions pertaining to the Thomas case. As I leaf through the hundreds of pages of legal documents, I come across several petitions written since Thomas's incarceration in 1982, each one listing a more recent date. All the petitions are signed by Zachariah Thomas, and a few of them are co-signed by his mother. They are requests for a new trial based upon what the petitioner claims was inadequate representation by his defense attorneys during his 1982 case. Detailed complaints list the numerous charges made by Thomas accusing his lawyer of being inept and substandard. Written in impressive legalese, these documents are hard to imagine as having been written by Thomas himself. However, each petition bears his signature and each is stamped with a large black "DENIED" on the front page and signed by a judge.

I have no doubt that the man in prison is the man who committed the crime. I saw his picture and Paul recognized him on the stand, his face was marked by acne scars and bizarre, almost ritualistic cuts. It would have been nearly impossible to mistake somebody else for him. It amazes me that he has been so dogged in his petitioning for another trial, implying that he wasn't given his fair shake. And then I realize that perhaps many criminals survive in the prison system because they are able to convince themselves that they didn't commit the crimes for which they were convicted and that petitioning the court for a new trial was one of the rote rituals in a maximum security prison.

Of course I can't help wondering what Catherine would think if she knew that for all these years since his conviction Thomas has been requisitioning the court for a new trial. I feel fairly certain that if I didn't know anything, neither did she. It makes me uneasy to think that some judge somewhere along the line might take pity on his case and retry it. The idea of having to trot out the cast of players once again for another few weeks in court is unimaginable.

I fly back to New York with reams of notes and xerox copies of articles about police corruption as well as necessary documents about the rape case to begin pondering it all with the hope of writing about it. Not even a few hours after I walk into my apartment, I get a call from the public affairs office at Angola.

"Mr. Raine, this is Ronnie Smith. I'm the woman you've been speaking to about Zachariah Thomas."

"You don't need to introduce yourself. I know who you are."

"Well, that's good Mr. Raine. And that's how I like to live my life. People knowing who I am," she says, as sarcasm and hostility thicken her drawl. "Now you tole me you from New Orleans, right?" she says, pronouncing "Orleans" with three syllables.

"Yes, that's correct."

"Well, maybe down in New Orleans people don't feel the way I do."

This line of conversation has me completely flummoxed. "I don't understand," I say finally.

"I know you don't. And I didn't understand until I found out that you were one of Zachariah Thomas's victims."

Her voice is now seething and I realize that this bit of information is going to become a big obstacle in my going farther.

"Yes, I was. I mean I am."

"Well, Mr. Raine, don't you think you should've told us that. When you were making arrangements to try and do your interview?"

"Well now that you mention it I suppose I should have."

"Son, you playing the innocent with me?" the woman asks.

"I never interviewed anybody in prison before. And I assumed I had given you whatever information you needed."

"And I suppose I should believe that, too?"

"Look, I'm sorry that I didn't tell you."

"And who's to say that you don't have it in for Mr. Thomas? For all I know, you could be a nut yourself trying to get in here to go after him."

"How could I possibly do that?" I said. "In a maximum security prison?"

Her voice now rises to a fevered pitch. "People have ways. People try to pull things over on us all the time. Now there's no way you're getting in here for an interview. Unless Mr. Thomas says he'll see you. And once he finds out that you were one of his victims, you won't have a prayer."

Ten

"THIS IS EXACTLY ONE of the reasons why we're moving to Vanillaville," Catherine says, referring to a planned community in a small town in Texas. "It's sterile, but it's safe."

It is the spring of 1998 and Catherine and I are in her car, driving to a compound of buildings that her parents bought many years ago as an investment and renovation project. After years of family life in the suburbs, they then moved back to one of the roughest neighborhoods in New Orleans. They had hoped that their new community, wracked by poverty and filled with decaying architectural gems, would slowly turn around once they'd taken the lead by renovating these several buildings in a square block. But the neighborhood had not followed suit, and they'd ended up several years later living in a beautifully manicured, club-like compound of themselves and young professional tenants, an island-like anomaly among ramshackle family dwellings and threadbare convenience stores.

With much trepidation, I'd recently told Catherine that I'd been writing about the night in Audubon Park and now have just gingerly broached the news that Zachariah has been petitioning the court for a new trial.

"It's really no surprise, " she remarks cynically, after announcing that she and her family are moving to Texas. "I wouldn't be surprised if my father has been writing his own petitions to the court, making sure he does what he can to keep him in jail."

Happily married for ten years, Catherine now has two elementary school-aged children and a modest suburban house in the same community where we all grew up. Despite her aura of maintaining the suburban status quo, which I know she has opted for out of her desire for normalcy, I still have an indelible image of her as the same free-spirited girl who loved to shirk responsibilities, who had endeared herself to us all that day when she had gone sailing and forgotten to attend her high school graduation and who, when she was a teenager, once showed up at her job as a catering waitress having forgotten her shoes, but ready to work at a high-end affair for a local politician. She has quickly made it clear to me that behind all the frontage of a nuclear family still lurks the same frightened woman who wonders if she gave off something particular that caused a man to attack her.

"Well," I say. "You don't have to go to that extreme, to moving to another place. I don't get a sense that he'll be granted a trial or that he'll get out anytime soon."

Catherine shakes her head. "I'm not taking any chances. With him or anybody else. I worry about the safety of my kids all the time. Even when they're in school. I want to be as safe as possible. I'm ready to get out of New Orleans. I'll feel a lot better going to the boring outskirts of Houston."

I wonder if such a constant preoccupation with the possibility of some violent act erupting in her world perhaps has kept Catherine from fully contemplating my news that I am writing about that night in Audubon Park. The build-up to telling her has certainly not been easy. I have long been afraid that she might react poorly to the idea, that in such writing I might be exposing a painful episode of her life.

"No, I wouldn't mind talking to you about it at all," she'd said. "I think so much of what happened then was never addressed, swept away, and I think it's necessary to re-remember parts of it. Like it or not, it shaped all of us, and probably in ways we aren't even aware of."

And now she is taking me to visit her parents whom she's told about my project and who would like to see me.

We finally arrive at the compound of nineteenth-century former slave-quarters buildings. In recent years, such structures, ubiquitous in New Orleans, are prized for their valuable period architectural details and sound construction and have become fashionable for those looking to renovate old houses. Catherine has explained to me that her parents bought the large property for a song, thinking they'd beat the swell of gentrification cresting in certain parts of the city where the shotgun architecture with high ceilings and huge windows lends itself to exquisite renovation. Hugh has always been a risk taker and hardly gave a second thought to the idea that he was moving from a safe suburban neighborhood to a run-down section of New Orleans where violent crime and robberies occurred frequently and where the sounds of gunfire often echo from the nearby battlegrounds of public housing projects just a few blocks away.

Catherine now explains that not long after her parents moved into their house, two men broke in while they were asleep. Her mother was the one who'd awakened and heard them and immediately told Hugh, who walked quietly down the hallway and distinctly overheard two voices in the adjacent bedroom calmly discussing what were the best things in the house for them to pilfer. When he threw the light on, two big guys lunged at him, and one of them had a knife. The three of them struggled all the way down the hallway and then they all rolled head over heels down the stairs. Somehow Hugh managed to extricate himself from the tangle, and ran to his desk where he kept a loaded gun. He started firing and killed one of the intruders on the spot and managed to wound the other one, who crashed through a closed French door and escaped.

Catherine has grown quiet. Finally she turns to me with a puzzled look on her face. "You might find this strange in light of everything you and I have been through, but after that night those guys broke in and when one of them died, my dad became depressed over it. The guy who died was young, in his twenties. My dad for a long time was preoccupied about what the guy's life could've been like. You would've thought he'd be all self-righteous about somebody daring to invade his territory. Then, a few years later, he was up on the roof doing some work and he fell off. Got a concussion. Almost died. But after he pulled through, we nicknamed him the Miracle Man because no one thought he would ever recover."

Now in his early seventies, Hugh has lost a great deal of weight. Though still handsome and dignified, he has changed dramatically in fifteen years. I can't help wondering if this might be due to the near-death injury as well as shooting the robber, an incident that, in retrospect, Catherine seemed to have so matter-of-factly described. I think back to the days when our families were tilling the community garden and when Hugh would show up, spiffy and youthful and vital in his tennis whites, contrasting with my father whose health already had begun failing him and who seemed like an aging man in comparison. Within five minutes of my arrival he is telling me, at my prompting, about his fall while repairing his house's steeply pitched roof, indicating the height which I reckon to be equal to a three-story building. "My father had a big fall, too," I find myself telling him.

"Coincidence, maybe?" he asks, squinting against the sun, more wrinkles blooming on his handsome, weathered face. After a moment of further reflection, Hugh asks, "Lose any of his senses?"

"Confidence. Does that count?" I ask.

Hugh laughs. "Not really. Everybody loses their confidence eventually." His voice trails off into distraction, and I know he is referring to himself. "In my case, after I fell I lost my sense of taste and smell."

"Yes, Catherine mentioned that," I say.

"She probably thinks it's all in my head, so to speak," he says with a laugh. "But that's why I've lost so much weight. Because of the fall, the brain damage it did, I can't taste anything anymore. No matter what I eat, the best gourmet food, it all tastes like plaster of Paris. And the best wine tastes like water."

Now Hugh takes me on a tour of the property, showing me all the out buildings, which they have renovated in order to enhance the feeling of a compound. When he thinks aloud about how many children he has and how they could all find room to live in the compound if they wanted to, my own memory flash of a long-ago desire to have been his surrogate child embarrasses me and strikes me to have been such a youthful folly.

"Catherine tells me you're doing some editing and writing," he mentions to me. "Good for you."

"She tell you what it's about?"

"Somewhat. That you're writing about violent crime and its effect on people. And writing about what happened to you and her."

"That's part of it," I say, preparing myself to explain the specifics that involve him and his family.

"Catherine says you've been trying to interview Zachariah Thomas?"

"Yeah, but Angola found out who I was and got mad, thought I was trying to put something over on them, and said they were pretty sure he wouldn't talk to me."

Hugh turns to me, puzzled. "What's the point? What would you say to him, anyway?"

I shrug. "I don't know. Maybe just hear his side of the story. After all he was never questioned in court."

"I wouldn't do it," he says. "I think you'd only open up Pandora's box."

"I've thought the same thing. Anyway, if I can't get in to see him, then all this speculating is moot."

Hugh nods. And then he turns to me, his face full of uncertainty. My relative youth and his relative old age seem to have forged a kind of respect that many other men of his ilk might have been unwilling to begrudge me. "I just want you to know," he says, "that a lot of my feelings about crime and responsibility have changed since that night that Catherine . . . well, you know what I'm saying." He stops and gazes up at the roof, as if flagging the place where he lost his balance and then his ability to taste. "Did Catherine tell you about the attempted robbery?"

"Yes."

Hugh shakes his head. "The boy I shot was only 25. After he died, I found out that he was terribly misguided and that circumstances and life were really against him from the start. And then I realized . . . you know I could've just stayed in bed, pretended I was asleep and let them rob us. But in those days I felt that I had to protect our house by facing those guys head-on. Hell, I could've gotten myself and my wife killed." He pauses, reflectively. "And I ended up killing somebody else. Somebody who probably would've been caught. What I did was crazy, rolling down the stairs. I guess I never really thought about it, I just acted." He turns to me now, his eyes squinting against the late afternoon sun.

And I say to him, "Do you think Zachariah Thomas would do a lot to get the blood off his hands?"

"Probably not. But I've stopping caring whether or not he's granted a new trial."

In the silence that ensues he ends up smiling. "So you're going to be a writer, huh?"

"Trying. I've published some things, but I am far from famous."

"Famous?" he pronounces the word with disdain. "Wouldn't complain about that," he admonishes me. "Wanting fame is one thing. Being famous is another, and no one should ever want to be famous. Becoming famous is one of the worst things that could happen to anyone. Anonymity is a gift, in the same way being able to play an instrument is a gift. Why would you want to lose precious privacy and anonymity?"

Hugh is playing his old role as the philosopher, with his view of the way life should be lived at the ready. I don't necessarily agree with what he is saying, but I feel no need to argue or contradict him. I just listen.

But there was something he was right about many years ago, something he had said to me once and which I have tried to live by ever since. I realize that his influence, short-lived as it was, had propelled me to break from New Orleans and venture to places beyond the river. Nearly twenty years earlier, the night before we went to Audubon Park, when Catherine and I had sat with him on the floor in the kitchen, he was strumming the guitar, encouraging us to have as many experiences as possible, to "drink deep from the well." Little did he know that, within twenty-four hours, a man would shoot up heroin and then accost his daughter whose life would never be the same.

As Hugh and I walk back to where his wife and Catherine are standing, I imagine myself finally gaining permission to visit Angola State prison, finally confronting Zachariah Thomas on the other side of a bulletproof glass wall. They have explained who I am and he has actually consented to see me—perhaps out of curiosity.

As I enter the narrow chamber with a handful of other visitors, I recognize him sitting in a chair, half slumped over. Forty-years-old, he will have aged prematurely from years of incarceration, from all the stints of solitary confinement that he has been forced to serve for further acts of brutality on his fellow inmates. When I sit down in front of him, he immediately will ask who I am and hesitating a moment I will tell him "one of your victims."

Each of us breathing rapidly, we are looking hard at one another, not as accuser and accused but as two men made safe from one another by an inviolable partition. A bit startled by my candor he will frown and then smile—that harrowing smile that once crossed his face when the thought of killing us was a mere whimsy, that smile that rippled when he drove past us in the Chrysler Cordoba. "I don't know you," he'll say. "First I've ever seen you. I'm innocent. You've got the wrong guy."

Now I think to myself, well maybe he really wouldn't remember me. Maybe I had to become a non-entity, unidentifiable in order for him to commit his gleeful act of violence. Since then, a great deal of history has intervened: I moved away from New Orleans years ago, and he entered the labyrinth of a prison system. Our meeting again after so much time has passed takes place in a completely different landscape, far from New Orleans and where the river bends. And what I finally come to at the end is this: that finding an act of contrition, seeking a final reckoning from Zachariah Thomas, is impossible. There is merely my own reckoning in what is written here. And what is written here can never be complete because the mystery at its core can never be explained.

ACKNOWLEDGMENTS

I would like to thank: Margaret Edwards for her astute suggestions; Sloan Harris, for taking a chance on me; Joyce Carol Oates and Ray Smith, for helping me shape my vision of the book; James Meyer, Gary Capetta, Nick Jones, and Martin Anker for friendship and encouragement; Lois Taylor for believing in me; Linda Bizzarro, for her compassion, legal expertise and intelligence; and Harriet Avery Brown for the right title.

I would especially like to thank my brother, Paul, who taught me to walk.

Bill Wright who, many years ago, made me think differently and see for the first time that the world was wide and full of possibilities.

And Joseph Olshan, for his love, support and dedication, and for his pushing me to write this book.